Austerity v

M000189178

Robert Skidelsky · Nicolò Fraccaroli

Austerity vs Stimulus

The Political Future of Economic Recovery

Robert Skidelsky
University of Warwick
Coventry, Warwickshire
UK

Nicolò Fraccaroli
London School of Economics
and Political Science
London, UK

ISBN 978-3-319-50438-4   ISBN 978-3-319-50439-1   (eBook)
DOI 10.1007/978-3-319-50439-1

Library of Congress Control Number: 2017937485

This Palgrave Macmillan imprint is published by Springer Nature
The registered company is Springer International Publishing AG
The registered company address is: Gewerbestrasse 11, 6330 Cham, Switzerland

Contents

List of Figures

Confidence Beyond Debt: The Role of Monetary Policy

Britain's Confidence

The Economic Consequences of Mr. Osborne

List of Tables

Introduction

It is known that the financial crisis of 2008 started as a subprime crisis. It is less known how it soon turned into a sovereign debt crisis, moving the focus of media and policy-makers from banks' balance sheets to governments' public debt. The Austerity vs Stimulus debate became prominent in this later phase.

Before 2008, American banks were issuing mortgages so easily that even the so-called subprime mortgage borrowers—borrowers with poor prospects of repayment—were accommodated with a loan. Once issued, banks put the loans in the financial market in the form of securities. When house prices started to fall, banks' balance sheets, largely inflated by the securities generated on mortgages, shrank. This is how the so-called subprime crisis begun. Fearing insolvency, banks stopped lending to each other and to their customers, causing a 'credit crunch'. This phenomenon, emerging at first in the USA, was soon transmitted to the financial markets in the UK and continental Europe, whose banks were interconnected with their American peers through the purchase of securities and interbank lending.

The German sociologist Wolfgang Streeck, whose essay opens this collection, described how the public sector intervened in the market to deal with this huge private debt problem. In order to restore confidence, governments bailed out their banks. This resulted in the explosion of public debt. Nevertheless, as soon as the financial sector was successfully rescued, the narrative of the Great Recession changed drastically. The crisis turned into a sovereign debt crisis, and the focal point of the discussion in newspapers, talk shows and even in academic debates, became the public debt problem. It was at this point that the arguments for austerity begun to gain success. Austerity policies aimed to restore fiscal balances. The restoration of fiscal balance was seen as the necessary condition for restoration of private sector confidence, and hence investment and economic growth.

The Reason for this Book

But why was austerity needed? This question is somewhat puzzling if we consider that 'before 2008 no one… [was]concerned with "excessive" national debts or deficits' as Mark Blyth, author of one of the most compelling books on the history of austerity, wrote.[1] Nevertheless, the issue divides contemporary economists, as is shown by the recent exchange in Project Syndicate between the economic historian Niall Ferguson (Harvard University) and one of the authors of this book, Robert Skidelsky (Warwick University), which inspired the creation of this short book.

To understand the full ramifications of the debate, one would need to delve deep into fiscal theory and historical arguments about the role of the state in the economy. Our aim here is more modest: not to describe how the 'dangerous idea' of austerity gained success among academics and policy-makers in the recent past (for which Blyth offers a persuasive account), but to offer a non-technical guide to a topic which dominates much of today's political discussion, and which even politicians lack the ability to discuss properly. (It is sufficient to note how many times British politicians talk about debt and deficit interchangeably).

The Puzzle

The question we are trying to answer in this book is: Should the British government have opted for austerity after the collapse of 2008? Or should it have gone for economic stimulus? Since austerity is the consensus policy in the European Union, the question is of more general relevance.

First, a couple of definitions: *austerity* is the reduction of the public deficit. In the UK its purpose was to restore private sector confidence in government finance, reduce the cost of government borrowing and free up resources in the private sector. On the Continent (Greece, Spain, Italy, Portugal, etc.), austerity was demanded as a condition for external financing of the deficit, its object being to eliminate the risk of default. Its medium-term purpose was to bring about a decrease in consumption and wages (known as 'internal devaluation'), in order to restore competitiveness and bring back growth. *Stimulus* is, on the contrary, an increase in the public deficit, aimed at sustaining aggregate demand and hence aggregate output and employment. At the end of the day, the final object of both stimulus and austerity policies is the same: to bring back growth. They differ, though, in the way they think this can be achieved, this difference reflecting a divergence in their view of how the economy works.

This divergence is not new. The debate, starting in 1924,[2] between the economist John Maynard Keynes and the officials of the British Treasury, already provides most of the answers we need today. The two stories, whose roots lie in history, represent divergent interpretations of the common understanding.

The Arguments for Austerity

Moral arguments for austerity, of which Florian Schui[3] has offered a wide review, can be found in pre-modern thinkers like Aristotle and Aquinas; economic arguments for austerity also have a long history.

The most familiar economic argument has been 'crowding out'—the view that government spending, whether financed by taxes or borrowing, diverts resources from productive use by the private sector. This goes back to Adam Smith and Ricardo. It was supported by the then Chancellor of the Exchequer, Winston Churchill, when he said in 1929:

> when the Government borrow[s] in the money market it becomes a new competitor with industry and engrosses itself resources which would otherwise have been employed by private enterprise, and in the process it raises the rent of money to all who have need of it.[4]

This reasoning is identical to that of contemporary austerians, like the Chicago economist John Cochrane, who wrote that 'every dollar of increased government spending must correspond to one less dollar of private spending. Jobs created by stimulus spending are offset by jobs lost from the decline in private spending. We can build roads instead of factories, but fiscal stimulus can't help us to build more of both'.[5]

Today the crowding out argument has taken a renewed form, known as 'expansionary fiscal contraction', elaborated by a group of academics belonging to the Bocconi University in Milan. According to Sue Konzelmann,[6] this proposition comes in two different, but complementary, forms.

The *Ricardian* school derives from Robert J. Barro's (Harvard) revision[7] of the concept of 'Ricardian equivalence', first stated by David Ricardo in his *Essay on the Funding System* (1820). Ricardian equivalence claims that a stimulus policy will fail to revive private spending, since forward-looking taxpayers know that a deficit today means higher taxes in the future, and will therefore increase their saving in order to pay the 'deferred taxes'. The net effect of increased borrowing is therefore zero.

The second school of thought is the *New Classical*. The claim here is that an increase in the government's deficit will raise interest rates, by reducing the total of saving available to finance private investment, and therefore increase the cost, and thus reduce the volume, of such investment. This thesis was supported by famous mainstream economists like the Nobel prizewinner Eugene Fama who claimed that 'stimulus plans absorb savings that would otherwise go to private investment. [...] Stimulus spending must be financed, which means it displaces other current uses of the same funds'.[8] Both arguments, it should be noted, assume an absence of spare productive capacity in the economy.

A refinement of the interest rate argument is so-called psychological crowding out, which introduces us to the main focus of this book: confidence. Those who believe in psychological crowding out concentrate on the psychological impact of deficits. The real effect of a bond-financed stimulus package remains the same: interest rates rise. Nevertheless, the cause is different. The reason for higher interest rates is not a shortage of savings, but a shortage of confidence of the business sector in the government's stimulus programme. John Maynard Keynes noticed this argument in the 1930s, when writing that a policy perceived by 'the average City man [...] as crack-brained and queer [...]' will 'upset the confidence of the business world and weaken its existing motives to action', without giving the government the time to 'put other motives in their place'.[9] This positive correlation between austerity and business confidence finds its origins in the Victorian theory of fiscal policy, in which a state's creditworthiness derives from a balanced budget (which included surpluses to repay the national debt). Accordingly, a reduction of public spending would have a positive effect on business' expectations, boosting private investment, while an increase in government spending, and especially borrowing, would shake the confidence of businessmen, who would reduce their spending. In the real world, though, it is extremely difficult to forecast business' reaction to fiscal policies. Helpless in face of the mismatch between economic theory and economic reality, Olivier Blanchard, the IMF's chief economist, called the business sector 'schizophrenic' for its reaction to austerity policies, which did not correspond to what mainstream theory suggested.

In 2011, an article by the Belgian economist Paul De Grauwe argued that confidence does not depend on the size of the national debt, by showing that the UK government, despite having a higher deficit and level of debt than Spain, was paying a lower interest rate on its debt.

A recent debate between Robert Skidelsky and Niall Ferguson also looked at the confidence question. Ferguson claimed that it is deficits which destroy confidence; Skidelsky replied that 'confidence closely tracks the performance of the economy. Austerity did not pull confidence up; it pushed it down, because it pushed the economy down'.[10] This intuition brings us directly to the main arguments of the Stimulus side.

The Arguments for Stimulus

The advocates of stimulus policies may loosely be called Keynesian. It is a myth that Keynes (or indeed post-war Keynesians) supported fiscal deficits at any time and under any circumstances. In the vulgarized view, Keynesian policies are associated with excessive and unbridled government spending to bribe the electorate. This incorrect interpretation of Keynes derives from one of his most quoted remarks that unemployment can be reduced 'if the Treasury were to fill old bottles with banknotes, bury them [...] and leave it to private enterprise [...] to dig the notes up again' (*General Theory*, p. 129): the continuation of the sentence 'if they can think of nothing better to do' is normally omitted. The tendency to frame the Austerity vs Stimulus debate as an endless contest between austerians and Keynesians is simply wrong.

Keynesians have never supported running budget deficits at all times. According to their view, the choice between expansive and restrictive fiscal policy depends entirely on the current economic conditions. In a phrase, less famous than the one above, Keynes wrote in 1937 that 'The boom, not the slump, is the right time for austerity at the Treasury'.

Keynes's reasoning was straightforward. During a boom, when the economy is at full employment, additional public expenditure would crowd out real resources. On the other hand, during a slump when the resources of an economy are under-employed, a deficit created through fiscal stimulus is not deferred taxation but a boost to economic activity. As such it creates its own means of repayment by increasing the aggregate income from which the government's revenue is drawn, and reducing the government's spending on unemployment. No question of 'crowding out' of real resources arises. Keynes did, however, recognize the possibility of psychological crowding out—that is adverse expectations by the business community concerning the effects of running deficits. He wrote the *General Theory*, in large part, to create expectations which would support what he believed to be the correct policy.

Relationship with Monetary Policy

Expansionary policy can take two forms, fiscal and monetary. In this book, we have concentrated on stimulus by fiscal measures. But the economy might also be stimulated by monetary policy. Indeed, both weapons were used in the immediate aftermath of the downturn. Attention then switched to the explosion of public sector deficits, and fiscal expansion to expand aggregate demand was ruled out on confidence grounds. But it was also recognized that austerity was hindering recovery. So, in both the UK and the Eurozone, the authorities sought to offset fiscal contraction by monetary expansion, through the 'unconventional' use of quantitative easing: the Bank of England purchased £350 billion in assets mainly government bonds, between February 2009 and October 2012. In March 2015, the European Central Bank (ECB) led by Mario Draghi started to buy €60 billion of assets every month. In this book, we will not pursue the debate concerning the efficacy of quantitative easing, or the interaction between monetary and fiscal policy, but reproduce an assessment by Thomas Fazi of the Draghi QE policy.

Austerity vs Stimulus: A Political Debate

As this introduction has already suggested, the revival of the debate was mainly driven by political factors. A recent letter on *The Guardian* signed by David Blanchflower, Mariana Mazzucato, Victoria Chick and others[11] argues that austerity has little to do with economic theory, the view also taken by Paul Krugman. Despite its origins in academia, the idea of austerity gained success mainly because of its political message. Austerity's political-economic prescription, in fact, matches the ideology of laissez-faire, a common ground for European and British centre-right parties that dominated the political scene before and during the recession (with the exception of the new labour). The idea that economic growth should come from the private sector and that government's fiscal policy should not interfere with the functioning of the market offered strong political support for policy-makers who wanted to reduce the size and influence of the state, an ideology for which Alesina and the other Bocconi scholars provided the needed (even if definitely scanty)[12] evidence.

Today stimulus ideas are spreading among new emerging left-wing forces in Europe, trying to break with the current narrative in which the state should act as an individual household, saving wisely and paying off its debt. While Keynesianism's original purpose was to 'save' the capitalist system (unable to adjust on its own), its prescriptions find a favourable response in left-wing parties, whose aim is to preserve the state's presence in the economy, and in particular to protect the social security system, the main target of austerity cuts. As Italian economist Giorgio La Malfa puts it in the conclusion of his most recent publication (*John Maynard Keynes*, 2015, Feltrinelli), Keynes's ideas could represent the next dividing line—what political scientists would call 'cleavage'—in the new European party-system emerging from the crisis. New forces such as Syriza in Greece, Podemos in Spain, the Bloco de Esquerda in Portugal today are headed in this direction. In the UK, the victory of Jeremy Corbyn as leader of the Labour party, being the only candidate who advocated deficit spending, suggests that this Keynesian trend is spreading to Westminster.

Politics aside, the outcome of the debate between Austerity and Stimulus will be settled (for the time being) by what is deemed to work. A quick return to a satisfactory 'normal' of growth and employment will seem to vindicate the Austerity school: indeed, Britain's chancellor, George Osborne, has already been claiming victory in the fiscal battle. Any undue prolongation of stagnation on the European continent, or a return to 'boom and bust' in Britain, will strengthen Austerity's challengers. The austerity story, though shaken, is today still the dominant one in Europe. As Robert Skidelsky put it, the 'Master' has yet to return.

Robert Skidelsky
Nicolò Fraccaroli

Notes

1. Mark Blyth (2013) *Austerity. The History of a Dangerous Idea*, Oxford: Oxford University Press.
2. With the publication on *Nation and Athenaeum* of Keynes's article 'Does Unemployment Need a Drastic Remedy?', in which the British economist argued that monetary policy was not enough to fight unemployment, but also fiscal stimulus was needed.
3. Florian Schui (2014) *Austerity. The Great Failure*, New Haven and London: Yale University Press.
4. Winston Churchill (1929) *Disposal of the Surplus*, Common Sitting of 15 April 1929, Series 5, vol. 227, Hansard.
5. Cochrane, J. (2009) *Fiscal Stimulus, Fiscal Inflation or Fiscal Fallacies?*, http://faculty.chicagobooth.edu/john.cochrane/research/Papers/fiscal2.htm.
6. Sue Konzelmann (2012) *The Economics of Austerity*, Centre for Business Research, University of Cambridge, WP No. 434.
7. Robert J. Barro (1979) *On the Determination of Public Debt*, Journal of Political Economy, 87 (5), 940–971.
8. Eugene Fama (2009) *Bailouts and Stimulus Plans*, Fama/French Forum, 13 January.https://www.dimensional.com/famafrench/essays/bailouts-and-stimulus-plans.aspx.
9. John Maynard Keynes, XXI, p. 290, quoted in Marcus Miller, Robert Skidelsky and Paul Weller (1990) *Fear of Deficit Financing: Is It Rational?*, in Roger Dornbusch and Mario Draghi (eds.) *Public Debt Management: Theory and History*, CEPR, Cambridge, UK: Cambridge University Press.
10. Robert Skidelsky (2015) *No Pain, No Gain for Britain?*, Project Syndicate, May 19. https://www.project-syndicate.org/debate/skidelsky-and-ferguson-debate-austerity#niall-ferguson-british-austerity-by-robert-skidelsky-2015-05.
11. David Blanchflower et al. (2015) Jeremy Corbyn's opposition to austerity is actually mainstream economics, The Guardian, 23 August 2015. http://www.theguardian.com/politics/2015/aug/23/jeremy-corbynsopposition-to-austerity-is-actually-mainstream-economics.
12. The title of one of the papers that inspired the theory of expansionary fiscal contraction is very eloquent in this regard: F. Giavazzi and M. Pagano (1990) *Can Severe Fiscal Contraction be Expansionary? Tales of Two Small European Countries*, NBER Working Paper n. 3372.

Part I

The Politics of the Debate

Austerity in the Tension Between Capitalism and Democracy

Original title: *The Crisis in Context: Democratic Capitalism and Its Contradictions.*
Published in the series of MPIfG Discussion Paper, n. 11/15, Cologne.

Wolfgang Streeck describes the history of postwar crises as the product of an inherent redistributive conflict in capitalist democracies: the bipolarized tension "between democratic claims for social justice and capitalist demands for distribution by marginal productivity." In the 1990s, Western governments were pressured by private creditors to reduce their debt (capitalist demands). At the same time, politicians were aware that austerity policies were adverse to the "democratic claims for social justice," as they were substantially aimed at cutting public services to those citizens that elected them. The compromise they found was what Colin Crouch (2009) called 'Privatized Keynesianism', that is the replacement of public debt with private debt. Through deregulation, it was easier for banks to issue credit to individuals, that could get through private loans, and therefore by indebting themselves, those services before guaranteed by the State, like education, health and so on. "Financial liberalization thus compensated for social policy being cut in an era of fiscal consolidation and public austerity," as

Streeck explains. But this solution was unsustainable in the long term, as the 'subprime crisis' has clearly shown. Private households could not pay back their loans to banks. Banks faced insolvency unless the state bailed them out. Streeck's analysis looks at austerity as a response by the government to market claims at the expenses of social rights; the rationale being the need to restore the market's confidence in the government, which will be a crucial element in the analysis of this book.

By **Wolfgang Streeck**

As the global financial system was about to disintegrate, nation-states had to restore economic confidence by socializing the bad loans licensed in compensation for fiscal consolidation. Together with the fiscal expansion necessary to prevent a breakdown of what the Germans call the Realökonomie, this resulted in a dramatic new increase in public deficits and public debt—a development that, it may be noted, was not at all due to frivolous overspending by opportunistic politicians as implied by public choice theories, or to misconceived public institutions as suggested by a broad institutional economics literature produced in the 1990s under the auspices of, among others, the World Bank and the IMF (for a representative collection see Poterba/von Hagen 1999[1]). [...] Political power was deployed to make future resources available for securing present social peace, in that states more or less voluntarily took upon themselves a significant share of the new debt originally created in the private sector, so as to reassure creditors. But while this effectively rescued the financial industry's money factories, reinstating in very short time their extraordinary profits, salaries and bonuses, it did not and could not prevent rising suspicions, on the part of the very same "financial markets" that had just been saved by national governments from the consequences of their own indiscretion, that in the process governments might have overextended themselves. Even with the global economic crisis far from over, creditors began vociferously to demand a return to sound money through fiscal austerity, in search for reassurance that their vastly increased investment in government debt will not be lost.

[...]

Financial markets have since the crisis returned to charging different states widely different interest rates, thereby differentiating the pressure they apply on governments to make their citizens acquiesce with unprecedented spending cuts in line, again, with a basically unmodified market logic of distribution. In fact, given the amount of debt carried by most states today, even minor increases in the rate of interest on government bonds could cause fiscal disaster. At the same time, markets must avoid states declaring sovereign bankruptcy, which states always can do if market pressures become too strong. This is why other states have to be found that are willing to bail out those most at risk, in order to protect themselves from a general increase in interest rates on government bonds once the first state has defaulted. Solidarity, if one can call it this, between states in the interest of investors is also fostered where sovereign default would hit banks located outside the defaulting country, which might force the banks' home countries once again to nationalize huge amounts of bad debt in order to stabilize their economies. There are still more facets to the way in which the tension in democratic capitalism between demands for social rights and the workings of free markets currently expresses itself today. Some governments, foremost among them the Obama administration, are making desperate attempts to generate renewed economic growth through even more debt—in the hope of future consolidation policies, should they become inevitable, being assisted by a sizeable growth dividend. Others may be secretly hoping for a return to inflation melting down accumulated debt by softly expropriating creditors—which would, like economic growth, mitigate the political tensions to be expected from austerity. At the same time, financial markets as well as academic economists may be looking forward to an...even more than ever promising fight against political interference with the forces of the market, once and for all reinstating market discipline and putting an end to all political attempts to subvert it. Further complications arise from the fact that financial "markets," whoever they may be, need government debt for safe investment, and pressing too hard for balanced budgets may deprive them of highly desirable investment opportunities. The middle classes of the rich countries in particular have put a good part of their savings into government bonds, not to mention workers now heavily invested in supplementary pensions. Balanced budgets would likely mean that states would have to take from their middle classes, in the form of higher taxes, what these now can save and invest, among other things in public debt. Not only would citizens no longer collect interest, but they would also cease to be able to pass their savings on to their children. However, while this should make them interested in states being, if not debt-free, then reliably able to fulfill their obligations to their creditors, it may mean that they would have to pay for their government's liquidity in the form of deep cuts in public benefits and services on which they also, in part, depend. At the end of the day, however complicated the cross-cutting cleavages between the various interests in the emerging new field of the international politics of public debt may be, the price for financial stabilization is likely to be paid by those other than the owners of money, or at least of real money. For example, public pension reform will be accelerated by fiscal pressures at home and abroad, and to the extent that governments default anywhere in the world, private pensions will be hit as well. The average citizen will pay—for the consolidation of public finances, the bankruptcy of foreign states, the rising rates of interest on the public debt and, if eventually necessary and still possible, for another rescue of national and international banks—with his or her private savings, with cuts in public entitlements, with reduced public services and, one way or other, with higher taxes.

In the four decades since the end of postwar growth, the epicenter of the tectonic tension inside the political economy of democratic capitalism has migrated from one institutional location to the next, in the course giving rise to a sequence of different but systematically related economic disturbances. In the 1970s the conflict between democratic claims for social justice and capitalist demands for distribution by marginal productivity played itself out primarily in national labor markets where trade union wage pressure under politically guaranteed full employment caused accelerating inflation. When what was in effect redistribution by debasement of the currency became economically unsustainable, forcing governments under high political risks to put an end to it, the conflict reemerged in the electoral arena. Here it gave rise to growing disparity between public spending and public revenues and, as a consequence, to rapidly rising public debt, in response to voter demands for benefits and services in excess of what a democratic-capitalist economy could be made to hand over to its "tax state" (Schumpeter [1918]1991[2]). Just like inflation, conflict management by deficit spending could not continue forever. When efforts to rein in public debt became unavoidable, however, they had to be accompanied, for the sake of social peace, by financial deregulation easing access to private credit as an alternative route to accommodating normatively popular and politically powerful demands of citizens for security and prosperity. This, too, lasted not much longer than a decade until the global economy almost faltered under the burden of unrealistic promises of future payment for present consumption and investment, licensed by governments in compensation for fiscal austerity. Since then, the clash between popular ideas of social justice and economic insistence on market justice has once again changed sites, re-emerging this time in international capital markets and the complex contests currently taking place there between financial institutions and electorates, governments, states and international organizations. Now the issue is how far states can and must go in enforcing on their citizens the property rights and profit expectations of those that call themselves "the markets," so as to avoid having to declare bankruptcy while protecting as best they can what may still remain of their democratic legitimacy. Toleration of inflation, acceptance of public debt, and deregulation of private credit were no more than temporary stopgaps for governments confronted with an apparently irrepressible conflict between the two contradictory principles of allocation under democratic capitalism: social rights on the one hand and marginal productivity, as determined by the relationship between supply and demand, on the other. Each of the three worked for a while until they began to cause more problems than they solved, indicating that a lasting reconciliation of social and economic stability in capitalist democracies is no more than a utopian project. Eventually, all that governments were able to achieve in dealing with the crises of their day was to move them to new arenas where they reappeared in new forms. There is no reason to believe that the successive manifestation of the contradictions inherent in democratic capitalism in ever new varieties of economic disorder should today be at an end.

Notes

1. Poterba, James M./Jürgen von Hagen (1999) *Institutions, Politics and Fiscal Policy*, Chicago, IL: University of Chicago Press.
2. Schumpeter, Joseph A. ([1918]1991) *The Crisis of the Tax State*, in Richard Swedberg (ed.), *The Economics and Sociology of Capitalism*, Princeton, NJ: Princeton University Press, 99–141.

Part II

The Two Sides of the Debate

As it was anticipated in the introduction, the Austerity vs Stimulus debate is not new to the world of political economy. The best known historical example of it, is the clash of ideas between John Maynard Keynes and the officials of the British Treasury in the 1920s, the former supporting a stimulus plan in opposition to the austerity policies pursued by the latter. Here we propose a less famous exchange, between two sets of economists: a letter by Keynes (and others) published on The Times and the reply by the Austrian economist Friedrich von Hayek (together with other LSE professors) in 1932. Keynes and Pigou argued that lack of confidence in the private sector was leading to be "pile[d] up in bank balances". Only a fiscal stimulus could release the resources needed to revive the economy. Hayek and the other LSE academics replied that such policies would raise interest rates. The government should avoid any increases public expenditure (since it "imposes frictions and obstacles to readjustment"), and focus instead on supply-side reforms.

Keynes Vs Hayek

Keynes Vs Hayek—Part I

Original title: *Money for Productive Investment*
Published on *The Times* on October 17, 1932 (p. 13)

By **John Maynard Keynes et al**.

To the Editor of the Times.

Sir,

On October 10 you gave prominence in your columns to a letter inviting the opinion of economists on the problem of private spending. There are a large number of economists in this country and nobody can claim to speak for all of them. The signatories of this letter have, however, in various capacities, devoted many years to the consideration of economic problems. We do not think that many of our colleagues would disagree with what we are about to say.

In the period of the War it was patriotic duty for private citizens to cut their expenditure on the purchase of consumable goods and services

© The Author(s) 2017
R. Skidelsky and N. Fraccaroli, *Austerity vs Stimulus*,
DOI 10.1007/978-3-319-50439-1_2

to the limit of their power. Some sorts of private economy were, indeed, more in the national interest than others. But, in some degree, all sorts of economy set free resources—man-power, machine-power, shipping-power—for use by the Government directly or indirectly in the conduct of the War. Private economy implied the handing over of these resources for a vital national purpose. At the present time, the conditions are entirely different. If a person with an income of £1000, the whole of which he would normally spend, decides instead to save £500 of it, the labour and capital that he sets free are not passed over to an insatiable war machine. Nor is there any assurance that they will find their way into investment in new capital construction by public or private concerns. In certain cases, of course, they will do this. A landowner who spends £500 less than usual in festivities and devotes the £500 to building a barn or a cottage, or a business man who stints himself of luxuries so that he can put new machinery into his mill, is simply transferring productive resources from one use to another. But, when a man economizes in consumption, and lets the fruit of his economy pile up in bank balances or even in the purchase of existing securities, the released real resources do not find a new home waiting for them. In present conditions their entry into investment is blocked by lack of confidence. Moreover, private economy intensifies the block. For it further discourages all those forms of investment—factories, machinery, and so on—whose ultimate purpose is to make consumption goods. Consequently, in present conditions, private economy does not transfer from consumption to investment part of an unchanged national real income. On the contrary, it cuts down the national income by nearly as much as it cuts down consumption. Instead of enabling labour-power, machine-power and shipping-power to be turned to a different and more important use, it throws them into idleness.

Conduct in the matter of economy, as of most other things, is governed by a complex of motive. Some people, no doubt, are stinting their consumption because their incomes have diminished and they cannot spend so much as usual; others because their incomes are expected to diminish and they dare not do so. What it is in any individual's private interest to do and what weight he ought to assign to that private interest as against the public interest, when the two conflict, it is not for us to judge.

But one thing is, in our opinion, clear. The public interest in present conditions does not point towards private economy; to spend less money than we should like to do is not patriotic.

Moreover, what is true of individuals acting singly is equally true of groups of individuals acting through local authorities. If the citizens of a town wish to build a swimming-bath, or a library, or a museum, they will not, by refraining from doing this, promote a wider national interest. They will be "martyrs by mistake," and, in their martyrdom, will be injuring others as well as themselves. Through their misdirected good the mounting wave of unemployment will be lifted still higher.

We are your obedient servants,

D.H. MacGregor (Professor of Political Economy in the University of Oxford)
A.C. Pigou (Professor of Political Economy in the University of Cambridge)
J.M. Keynes
Walter Layton
Arthur Salter
J.C. Stamp

Keynes Vs Hayek—Part II

Original title: *Spending and Saving*
Published on *The Times* on Oct 19, 1932 (p. 10)

By **Friedrich von Hayek et al**.

To the Editor of the Times.

Sir,

The question whether to save or whether to spend which has been raised in your columns, is not unambiguous. It involves three separate issues: (1) Whether to use money or whether to hoard it; (2) whether to spend money or whether to invest it; and (3) whether Government investment is on all fours with investment by private individuals. While we do not wish to over-stress the nature of our differences with those of our professional colleagues who have already written to you on these subjects, yet on certain points that difference is sufficiently great to make the expression of an alternative view desirable.

1. On the first issue—whether to use one's money or whether to hoard it—there is no important difference between us. It is agreed that hoarding money, whether in cash or in idle balances, is deflationary in its effects. No one thinks that deflation is in itself desirable.
2. On the question whether to spend or whether to invest our position is different from that of the signatories [Pigou, Keynes et al.] of the letter which appeared in your columns on Monday. They appear to hold that it is a matter of indifference as regards the prospects of revival whether money is spent on consumption or on real investment. We, on the contrary, believe that one of the main difficulties of the world today is a deficiency of investment—a depression of the industries making for capital extension, etc., rather than of the industries making directly for consumption. Hence we regard a revival of investment as peculiarly desirable. The signatories of the letter referred to, however, appear to deprecate the purchase of existing securities on the ground that there is no guarantee that the money will find its way into real investment. We cannot endorse this view. Under modern conditions the security markets are an indispensable part of the mechanism of investment. A rise in the value of old securities is an indispensable preliminary to the flotation of new issues. The existence of a lag between the revival in old securities and revival elsewhere is not questioned. But we should regard it as little short of a disaster if the public should infer from what has been said that the purchase of existing securities and the placing of deposits in building societies, etc., were at the present time contrary to public interest or that the sale of securities or the withdrawal of such deposits would assist the coming recovery. It is perilous in the extreme to say anything which may still further weaken the habit of private saving.

But it is perhaps on the third question—the question whether this is an appropriate time for State and municipal authorities to extend their expenditure—that our difference with the signatories of the letter is most acute. On this point we find ourselves in agreement with your leading article on Monday. We are of the opinion that many of the troubles of the world at the present time are due to imprudent borrowing and spending on the part of the public authorities. We do not desire to see a renewal of such practices. At best they mortgage the Budgets of the future, and they tend to drive up the rate of interest—a process which is surely particularly undesirable at this juncture, when the revival of the supply of capital to private industry is an admitted urgent necessity. The depression has abundantly shown that the existence of public debt on a large scale imposes frictions and obstacles to readjustment very much greater than the frictions and obstacles imposed by the existence of private debt. Hence we cannot agree with the signatories of the letter that this is a time for new municipal swimming baths, etc., merely because people "feel they want" such amenities.

If the Government wish to help revival, the right way for them to proceed is, not to revert to their old habits of lavish expenditure, but to abolish those restrictions on trade and the free movement of capital (including restrictions on new issues) which are at present impeding even the beginning of recovery.

We are, Sir, your obedient servants,

T.E. Gregory, Cassel Professor of Economics
F.A. von Hayek, Tooke Professor of Economic Science and Statistics
Arnold Plant, Cassel Professor of Commerce
Lionel Robbins, Professor of Economics

University of London, Oct. 18.

Contemporary Arguments for Austerity

The concept of austerity was revived by a group of Italian graduates at Bocconi University in Milan. According to Mark Blyth, author of a book on the history of austerity,[1] the "modern argument for austerity" was developed by this group of scholars, of which the two most prominent members is Alberto Alesina (Harvard University, former Bocconi graduate), the author of the following article. In Blyth's words, "the importance of Alesina and his collaborators' work in defining and defending the modern policy case for austerity cannot be overestimated" (2013, p. 167). Therefore, in order to understand the position of the austerity-side, we started with a piece by the main exponent of the so-called "Bocconi school", where he exposes the main arguments of the expansionary fiscal contraction theory. The core intuition is that in time of crisis restrictive fiscal policies (public spending reduction or taxing) can have an expansionary effect, boosting GDP, in contrast to the Keynesian theory for which only countercyclical policies—i.e. Expansionary (restrictive) policies during a recession (boom)—can revive the economy. More precisely, according to Alesina, the optimal fiscal contraction during a recession should rely on spending cuts rather than increasing taxes. The strength of these findings lies on the massive

© The Author(s) 2017
R. Skidelsky and N. Fraccaroli, *Austerity vs Stimulus*,
DOI 10.1007/978-3-319-50439-1_3

empirical data they are based on: "a sample of 21 countries from 1970 to the most recent period". Nevertheless, data do not always display a definite "truth": as the IMF's critique to the theory of expansionary austerity shows, the narrative on the effects of economic policies strongly depends on the methodological perspective adopted. Such empirical issues are also raised by Carmen Reinhart and Kenneth Rogoff, authors of the second article of this section. According to them, provided that data and econometric techniques do not tell us the whole story, we should still try to interpret the behaviour of some variables. This is the case of the relationship between the level of debt and GDP growth noticed by Reinhart and Rogoff: once debt-to-GDP overcomes the ceiling of 90%, growth "rates are roughly cut in half" (p. 573).[2] Needless to say that such findings, published in the aftermath of the crisis, supported austerity policies of spending-cuts with the aim of reducing governments' debt.

Some Evidence in Favour of Austerity

Original Title: *Fiscal Adjustments and the recession*
Published on *VoxEu* on November 12, 2010

By **Alberto Alesina**

Many European countries are engaged in large fiscal adjustments. The standard Keynesian view is that these adjustments will cause deep recessions especially if they occur on the spending side (see for example Krugman 2010). A lively literature initiated by a paper by Giavazzi and Pagano (1990) has uncovered "non-Keynesian" effects of large fiscal adjustments. The latest instalment of this line of research is a paper that I co-authored with Silvia Ardagna (Alesina and Ardagna 2010).

This literature reaches three conclusions.

- First, fiscal adjustments on the spending side are more likely to lead to a permanent stabilisation of the budget.
- Second adjustments on the spending side have lower cost in terms of lost output.

- Third, some, not all, adjustments on the spending side are not followed by a downturn even on impact.

This may be due to a confidence effect on consumers and investors or because monetary policy can be more expansionary when a fiscal adjustment is credible. Another reason may be that raising taxes would have negative supply-side effects on labour costs, labour supply, and investments. These supply-side effects do not apply to spending cuts, which, on the contrary, imply lower taxes in the future.

A recent chapter of the IMF's September 2010 *World Economic Outlook* (WEO) argues that these results are incorrect. Yet the rhetoric of the IMF study exaggerates the differences in their results and claims.

The WEO focuses on the second and third result, and it does not deal with the first. On the second result the WEO chapter agrees that tax increases are much worse for the economy than spending cuts. It says that this effect comes mainly from different reactions of monetary policy, but their claim of having identified separately all of these channels is overstated because interest rates, current and expected, and exchange rates are endogenous to both fiscal and monetary policy.

Regarding the third result, the WEO chapter in particular criticises a paper I co-wrote with Silvia Ardagna. In it we analysed how countries grow during the year of a fiscal adjustment, and in the two following years. The study covers a sample of 21 countries from 1970 to the most recent period and defines a fiscal adjustment as "expansionary" if GDP growth in the year of the adjustment, and in the two following years, is in the top 25% of the sample. To correct for the world business cycle, our study considers the growth of each country in difference from average G7 countries' growth. The main finding is that about one fifth of fiscal adjustment episodes are expansionary and these are based mostly on spending cuts.

Our definition of a fiscal adjustment relies on the cyclically adjusted primary balance; this is the standard methodology used in the literature to date. That is, the paper defines an adjustment when there is a large fall in the primary deficit (more than 1.5% of GDP) after taking out the effect of the cycle on the primary deficit. The idea is that such a sharp reduction of cyclically adjusted deficits in virtually all cases has to be the result of some policy action and not "business as usual". Indeed, such a measure leaves out what would be "incorrect" selections of episodes. For example, in the nineties in the US, there were no discretionary fiscal contractionary policies despite the sharp reduction of the deficit. In fact, the latter was due only to sustained growth of the economy. The deficit went down quickly, but the US is not defined as a case of expansionary fiscal adjustment because the cyclical correction reveals that it was the sustained growth of the economy that reduced the deficit, not policy actions. This method for cyclical adjustment is standard and widely used.

The imperfections of cyclical adjustments are well known, and this is shown in the vast literature on this subject experiments with many sensitive tests. Yet the WEO chapter simply dismisses this methodology. It claims to have found a better way of identifying when a fiscal adjustment really occurs. How? By reading IMF and OECD historical reports and checking what countries were intending to do at the time of publication. There are pros and cons in this approach. First, it involves many judgment calls. Second, and more importantly, the idea that this procedure would eliminate endogeneity (i.e., fiscal policy responding to the economy and not the other way around) is non tenable.

Certainly various governments cut taxes or spending programmes (or the other way around) for a reason, such as how the economy was doing or expected to be doing. The WEO chapter claims to have mirrored the methodology of Romer and Romer for the US economy. But this is not quite right. Romer and Romer examined a voluminous documentation of Congressional proceedings to disentangle "exogenous" tax changes, i.e. exogenous to the economic cycle. The WEO Chapter uses descriptive IMF and OECD reports which state what happens to the deficit in a particular period; these reports do not go into the details of policymakers' intentions, discussions and congressional records.

It is worth pointing out that many other papers using different methodologies have identified cases of expansionary fiscal adjustments. For example, in a previous paper we investigate, at length, nine specific episodes of fiscal adjustments, some of which expansionary and others contractionary (Alesina and Ardagna 1998). Giavazzi and Pagano (1990) had already discovered two expansionary episodes. In his published comments on that paper, Olivier Blanchard (the IMF's Chief Economist) argued that expansionary fiscal adjustments can indeed occur and he also showed why. He argued that a fiscal adjustment, by removing fear of future harsher ones and future taxes, can stabilise expectations, increase consumers' expected disposable income, and increase confidence of investors and therefore can stimulate private demand.

Below is an incomplete list of papers consistent with the possibility of expansionary fiscal adjustments. All of these analyses find two results:

- Spending cuts are less recessionary than tax increases when deficits are reduced, and;
- Sometimes, not always, some fiscal adjustments based upon spending cuts are not associated with economic downturns.

I don't believe that, despite its rhetoric, the WEO chapter proves that either of these two conclusions regarding the history of fiscal adjustments is incorrect.

What will happen to the current cases of budget cuts in an especially difficult situation for the world economy remains to be seen. But one thing is certain: Several European countries had no choice but to initiate fiscal adjustment programmes. Let's hope for the best.

Literature on Possibly Expansionary Fiscal Adjustments

Alesina A., and R. Perotti (1995), "Fiscal Expansions and Adjustments in OECD Countries, *Economic Policy*, n. 21, 207–247.

Alesina A., S. Ardagna, R. Perotti, and F. Schiantarelli (2002), "Fiscal Policy, Profits, and Investment", *American Economic Review*, vol. 92, no. 3, June 2002, 571–589.

Alesina A., R. Perotti, and J. Tavares (1998), "The Political Economy of Fiscal Adjustments", *Brookings Papers on Economic Activity*, Spring 1998.

Alesina and Ardagna (1998), "Tales of Fiscal Adjustments", *Economic Policy*, no. 27, October 1998, pp. 489–545.

Ardagna Silvia (2004), "Fiscal Stabilizations: When Do They Work and Why?", *European Economic Review*, vol. 48, No. 5, October 2004, pp. 1047–1074.

Blanchard, Olivier (1990), "Comments on Giavazzi and Pagano", *NBER Macroeconomic Annual.*

Broadbent, Ben and Kevin Daly (2010), "Limiting the fall-out from fiscal adjustment", Goldman Sachs, Global Economics Paper 195, April.

Cournede, B. and F. Gonand (2006), "Restoring Fiscal Sustainability in the Euro Area: Raise Taxes or Curb Spending?", OECD Economics Department Working Papers no. 520.

Giavazzi F., and M. Pagano (1990), Can Severe Fiscal Contractions Be Expansionary? Tales of Two Small European Countries, *NBER Macroeconomics Annual,* MIT Press, (Cambridge, MA), 1990, 95–122.

Guihard S., M. Kennedy, E. Wurzel, and C. Andre (2007), "What Promotes Fiscal Consolidation: OECD Country Experience", OECD Economics Department Working Papers no. 553.

Giavazzi F., and M. Pagano (1996), Non-Keynesian Effects of Fiscal Policy Changes: International Evidence and the Swedish Experience, *Swedish Economic Policy Review*, vol. 3, n. 1, Spring, 67–112.

McDermott J. and R. Wescott (1996), "An Empirical Analysis of Fiscal Adjustments", *IMF Staff papers,* 43(4): 723–753.

Lambertini, L and J Tavares (2005), "Exchange rates and fiscal adjustments: Evidence from the OECD and implications for the EMU", *Contributions to Macroeconomics*, 5, 11.

Tavares, J (2004), "Does right or left matter? Cabinets, credibility and fiscal adjustments", *Journal of Public Economics*, 88: 2447–2468.

von Hagen J and R Strauch, (2001), "Fiscal Consolidations: Quality, Economic Conditions, and Success, *Public Choice*, 109, 3–4: 327–346.

von Hagen J, AH Hallett, R Strauch (2002), "Budgetary Consolidation in Europe: Quality, Economic Conditions, and Persistence", *Journal of the Japanese and International Economics*, 16: 512–535.

Debt and Growth

Original Title: *Debt and Growth revisited*
Published on VoxEU on August 11, 2010

By **Carmen M. Reinhart** and **Kenneth S. Rogoff**

[…]

We studied economic growth and inflation at different levels of government and external debt (Reinhart and Rogoff 2010a). The public discussion of our empirical strategy and results has been somewhat muddled. Here, we attempt to clarify matters, particularly with respect to sample coverage (our evidence encompasses 44 countries over two centuries—not just the US), debt-growth causality (our book emphasises the bi-directional nature of the relationship), as well as nonlinearities in the debt-growth connection and thresholds evident in the data.

[…]

The Basic Exercise and Key Results

Our analysis was based on newly compiled data on 44 countries spanning about 200 years. This amounts to 3700 annual observations and covers a wide range of political systems, institutions, exchange rate arrangements, and historic circumstances.

The main findings of that study are:

- First, the relationship between government debt and real GDP growth is weak for debt/GDP ratios below 90% of GDP.[3] Above the threshold of 90%, median growth rates fall by 1%, and average growth falls considerably more. The threshold for public debt is similar in advanced and emerging economies and applies for both the

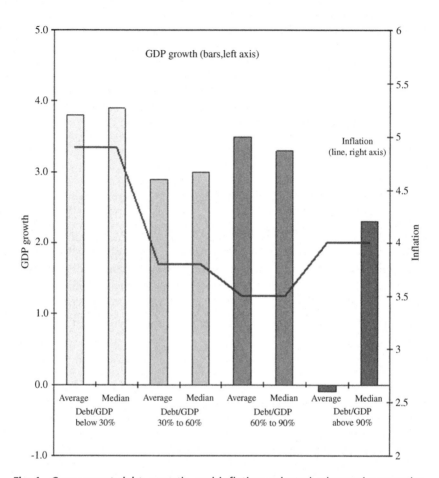

Fig. 1 Government debt, growth, and inflation: selected advanced economies, 1946–2009. *Notes* Central government debt includes domestic and external public debts. The 20 advanced economies included are Australia. Austria, Belgium, Canada, Denmark, Finland, France, Germany, Greece, Ireland, Italy, Japan, Netherlands, New Zealand, Norway, Portugal, Spain, Sweden, the UK, and the US. The number of observations for the four debt groups are: 443 for debt/GDP below 30%; 442 for debt/GDP 30–60%; 199 observations for debt/GDP 60–90%; and 96 for debt/GDP above 90%. There are 1180 observations. *Sources* Reinhart and Rogoff (2010a) and sources cited therein

post World War II period and as far back as the data permit (often well into the 1800s).

- Second, emerging markets face lower thresholds for total external debt (public and private)—which is usually denominated in a foreign currency. When total external debt reaches 60% of GDP, annual growth declines about 2%; for higher levels, growth rates are roughly cut in half.
- Third, there is no apparent contemporaneous link between inflation and public debt levels for the advanced countries as a group (some countries, such as the US, have experienced higher inflation when debt/GDP is high). The story is entirely different for emerging markets, where inflation rises sharply as debt increases.

Figure 1 summarises our main conclusions as they apply to the 20 advanced countries in our 44-country sample. We will concentrate here on the advanced countries, as that is where much of the public debate is centred.[4]

In the figure, the annual observations are grouped into four categories, according to the ratio of debt-to GDP during that particular year. Specifically years when debt-to-GDP levels were:

- below 30%;
- 30–60%;
- 60–90%; and
- above 90%.[5]

The bars show average and median GDP growth for each of the four debt categories. Note that of the 1186 annual observations, there are a significant number in each category, including 96 above 90%. (Recent observations in that top bracket come from Belgium, Greece, Italy, and Japan.)

From the figure, it is evident that there is *no* obvious link between debt and growth until public debt exceeds the 90% threshold. The observations with debt to GDP over 90% have median growth roughly

1% lower than the lower debt burden groups and mean levels of growth almost 4% lower. [...] The line in Fig. 1 plots the median inflation for the different debt groupings—which makes clear that there is *no* apparent pattern of *simultaneous* rising inflation and debt.

Table 1 Real GDP growth as the level of government debt varies: selected advanced economies, 1790–2009 (annual percent change)

Country	Period	Below 30%	30–60%	60–90%	90% and above
Australia	1902–2009	3.1	4.1	2.3	4.6
Austria	1880–2009	4.3	3.0	2.3	n.a.
Belgium	1835–2009	3.0	2.6	2.1	3.3
Canada	1925–2009	2.0	4.5	3 0	2.2
Denmark	1880–2009	3.1	1.7	2.4	n.a.
Finland	1913–2009	3.2	3.0	4.3	1.9
France	1880–2009	4.9	2.7	2.8	2.3
Germany	1880–2009	3.6	0.9	n.a.	n.a.
Greece	1884–2009	4.0	*0.3*	*4.8*	2.5
Ireland	1949–2009	4.4	4.5	4.0	2.4
Italy	1880–2009	*5.4*	*4.9*	1.9	0.7
Japan	1885–2009	4.9	3.7	3.9	0.7
Netherlands	1880–2009	4.0	2.8	2.4	2.0
New Zealand	1932–2009	2.5	2.9	3.9	*3.6*
Norway	1880–2009	2.9	4.4	n.a.	n.a.
Portugal	1851–2009	4.8	2.5	1.4	n.a.
Spain	1850–2009	*1.6*	3.3	*1.3*	2.2
Sweden	1880–2009	2.9	2.9	2.7	n.a.
United Kingdom	1830–2009	2.5	2.2	2.1	1.8
United States	1790–2009	4.0	3.4	3.3	−1.8
Average		**3.7**	**3.0**	**3.4**	**1.7**
Median		**3.9**	**3.1**	**2.8**	**1.9**
Number of observations = **2317**		866	654	445	352

Notes Anna denotes no observations were recorded for that particular debt range. There are missing observations, most notably during World War I and II years; further details are provided in the data appendices to Reinhart and Rogoff (2009) and are available from the authors. Minimum and maximum values for each debt range are shown in bolditalics

Sources Many sources, among the more prominent are: IMF, World Economic Outlook, OECD, World Bank, Global Development Finance. Extensive other sources are cited in Reinhart and Rogoff (2009)

High-Debt Episodes in the Sample

The episodes that attract our interest are those where debt levels were historically high. [...] It is common knowledge that the US emerged after World War II with a very high debt level. But this also held for Australia, Canada, and most markedly the UK, where public/debt GDP peaked at near 240% in 1948. These cases from the aftermath of World War II are joined in our sample by a number of peacetime high-debt episodes:

- the 1920s and 1980s to the present in Belgium,
- the 1920s in France,
- Greece in the 1920s,
- 1930s and 1990s to the present,
- Ireland in the 1980s,
- Italy in the 1990s,
- Spain at the turn of the last century,
- the UK in the interwar period and prior to the 1860s and, of course,
- Japan in the past decade.

As will be discussed, episodes where debt is above 90% are themselves rare and, as shown in Table 1, a number of countries have never had debt entries above 90%.

Debt Thresholds and Nonlinearities: The 90% Benchmark

Thresholds and non-linearities play a key role in understanding the relationship between debt and growth that should not be ignored in casual re-interpretations.

Thresholds

Those who have done data work know that mapping vague concepts like "high debt" or "overvalued exchange rates" into workable definitions requires arbitrary judgments about where to draw lines; there is no other way to interpret the facts and inform the discussion. In the case of debt, we worked with four data "buckets": 0–30%, 30–60%, 60–90%, and over 90%. The last one turned out to be the critical one for detecting a difference in growth performance, so we single it out for discussion here.

Figure 1 shows a histogram of public debt-to-GDP as well as pooled descriptive statistics (inset) for the advanced economies (to compliment the country-specific ones shown in Table 1) over the post World War II period. [...] About 92% of the observations fall *below* the 90% threshold. In effect, about 76% of the observations were below the 60% Maastricht criteria.

Put differently, our "high vulnerability" region for lower growth (the area under the curve to the right of the 90% line) comprises only about 8% of the sample population. [...]

If debt levels above 90% are indeed as benign as some suggest, one might have expected to see a higher incidence of these over the long course of history.

Certainly our read of the evidence, as underscored by the central theme of our 2009 book, hardly suggests that politicians are universally

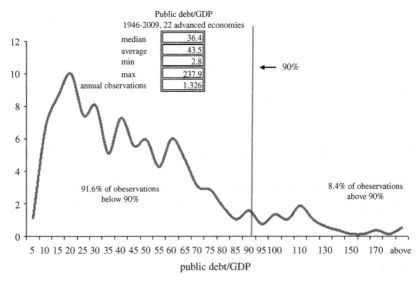

Fig. 2 The 90% debt/GDP threshold: 1946–2009, advanced economies. Probability density function. *Notes* The advanced economy sample is the complete IMF grouping (Switzerland and Iceland were added). It includes Australia. Austria, Belgium, Canada, Denmark, Finland, France, Germany, Greece, Iceland, Ireland, Italy, Japan, Netherlands, New Zealand, Norway, Portugal, Spain, Sweden, Switzerland, the UK, and the US. *Sources* Reinhart and Rogoff (2009, 2010a)

too cautious in accumulating high debt levels. Quite the contrary, far too often they take undue risks with debt build-ups, relying implicitly perhaps on the fact these risks often take a very long time to materialise. If debt-to-GDP levels over 90% are so benign, then generations of politicians must have been overlooking proverbial money on the street.

We do not pretend to argue that growth will be normal at 89% and subpar (about 1% lower) at 91% debt/GDP any more than a car crash is unlikely at 54 mph and near certain at 56 mph. However, mapping the theoretical notion of "*vulnerability regions*" to bad outcomes by necessity involves defining thresholds, just as traffic signs in the US specify 55 mph (these methodology issues are discussed in Kaminsky and Reinhart 1999) (Fig. 2).

Nonlinear Relationship

We summarised the results in our paper by writing:

> the relationship between government debt and real GDP growth is weak for debt/GDP ratios below a threshold of 90% of GDP. Above 90%, median growth rates fall by 1%, and average growth falls considerably more. (Reinhart and Rogoff 2010a)

Revisiting Fig. 1 is useful for illustrating the importance of nonlinearities in the debt-growth link. Simply put, for 92% of the observations in our sample there is no systematic link between debt and growth (Bruno and Easterly 1998 find similar results). Thus, if we did a simple scatter plot of all the observations on debt/GDP and on growth we might expect to find a "clouded mess." We can highlight this general point with the US case. As noted in the working paper version of Reinhart and Rogoff (2010a), for the period 1790–2009, there are a total of 216 observations of which 211 (or 98%) are below the 90% debt to GDP cutoff. It should be quite obvious that a scatter plot of the US data would not be capable of revealing a systematic pattern (as demonstrated in the work Iron and Bivens 2010). Indeed, this example illustrates one of our main results, that there is no systematic relationship between debt and growth below a threshold of 90% of GDP.

Debt and Growth Causality

As discussed, we examine average and median growth and inflation rates *contemporaneously* with debt. [...] Where do we place the evidence on causality? For low-to-moderate levels of debt there may or may not be one; the issue is an empirical one, which merits study. For high levels of debt the evidence points to *bi-directional* causality.

Growth-to-Debt

Our analysis of the aftermath of financial crisis Reinhart and Rogoff (2008) presents compelling evidence for both advanced and emerging markets over 1800–2008 on the fiscal impacts (revenue, deficits, debts, and sovereign credit ratings) of the recessions associated with banking crises; see Fig. 3.

As we sum up,

> Banking crises weaken fiscal positions, with government revenues invariably contracting. 3 years after a crisis central government debt increases by about 86%. The fiscal burden of banking crisis extends beyond the cost of the bailouts. (Reinhart and Rogoff 2008)

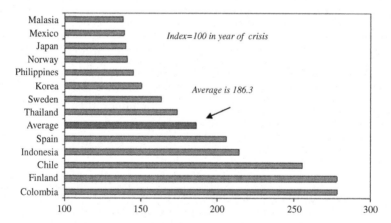

Fig. 3 Cumulative increase in public debt in the 3 years following the banking crisis. *Source* Reinhart and Rogoff (2008)

There is little room to doubt that severe economic downturns, irrespective whether their origins was a financial crisis or not, will, in most instances, lead to higher debt/GDP levels contemporaneously and or with a lag. There is, of course, a vast literature on cyclically-adjusted fiscal deficits making exactly this point.

Debt-to-Growth

A unilateral causal pattern from growth to debt, however, does not accord with the evidence. Public debt surges are associated with a higher incidence of debt crises. This temporal pattern is analysed in Reinhart and Rogoff (2010b) and in the accompanying country-by-country analyses cited therein.

In the current context, even a cursory reading of the recent turmoil in Greece and other European countries can be importantly traced to the adverse impacts of high levels of government debt (or potentially guaranteed debt) on county risk and economic outcomes. At a very basic level, a high public debt burden implies higher future taxes (inflation is also a tax) or lower future government spending, if the government is expected to repay its debts.

There is scant evidence to suggest that high debt has little impact on growth.

Kumar and Woo (2010) highlight in their cross-country findings that debt levels have negative consequences for subsequent growth, even after controlling for other standard determinants in growth equations. For emerging markets, an older literature on the debt overhang of the 1980s frequently addresses this theme.

Implications and Policy

One need look no further than the stubbornly high unemployment rates in the US and other advanced economies to be convinced how important it is to develop a better understanding of the growth prospects for the decade ahead. We have presented evidence—in a multi-country sample spanning about two centuries—suggesting that high levels of debt dampen growth. One can argue that the US can tolerate higher levels of debt than other countries without having its solvency called into question. That is probably so.[6]

We have shown in our earlier work that a country's credit history plays a prominent role in determining what levels of debt it can sustain without landing on a sovereign debt crisis. More to the point of this paper, however, we have no comparable evidence yet to suggest that the consequences of higher debt levels for *growth* will be different for the US than for other advanced economies. It is an issue yet to be explored. [...] Perhaps soaring US debt levels will not prove to be a drag on growth in the decades to come. However, if history is any guide, that is a risky proposition and over-reliance on US exceptionalism may only prove to be one more example of the "This Time is Different" syndrome.[7]

For many if not most advanced countries, dismissing debt concerns at this time is tantamount to ignoring the proverbial elephant in the room.

Notes

1. Blyth, M. (2013) *Austerity: The History of a Dangerous Idea*, Oxford: Oxford University Press (Blyth 2013).
2. The original article that contains the quote was published in 2010 on the American Economic Review. Full reference: Reinhart, Carmen M. and Kenneth S. Rogoff (2010a) 'Growth in a Time of Debt', *American Economics Review*, 100(2), 573–78.
3. In this paper "public debt" refers to gross central government debt. "Domestic public debt" is government debt issued under domestic legal jurisdiction. Public debt does not include obligations carrying a government guarantee. Total gross external debt includes the external debts of all branches of government as well as private debt that issued by domestic private entities under a foreign jurisdiction.
4. The comparable emerging market exercises are presented in the original paper.
5. The four "buckets" encompassing low, medium-low, medium-high, and high debt levels are based on our interpretation of much of the literature and policy discussion on what are considered low, high etc. debt levels. It parallels the World Bank country groupings according to four income

groups. Sensitivity analysis involving a different set of debt cutoffs merits exploration, as do country-specific debt thresholds along the broad lines discussed in Reinhart et al. (2003).

6. See also Reinhart and Reinhart (2007).

7. The "This Time is Different Syndrome" is rooted in the firmly-held beliefs that: (i) Financial crises and negative outcomes are something that happen to other people in other countries at other times (these do not happen here and now to us); (ii) we are doing things better, we are smarter, we have learned from the past mistakes; (iii) as a consequence, old rules of valuation are not thought to apply any longer.

References

Alesina, A., & Ardagna, S. (1998). Tales of fiscal adjustments. *Economic Policy, 13*(27), 488–545.

Alesina, A., & Ardagna, S. (2010). Large changes in fiscal policy taxes versus spending. In J. R. Brown (Ed.), *Tax policy and the economy*. Chicago: NBER and University of Chicago Press.

Blyth, M. (2013). *Austerity: The history of a dangerous idea*. Oxford: Oxford University Press.

Bruno, M., & Easterly, W. (1998). Inflation crises and long-run growth. *Journal of Monetary Economics, 41*(1), 3–26.

Giavazzi, F., & Pagano, M. (1990). Can Severe Fiscal Contractions Be Expansionary? *Tales of Two Small European Countries*, Cambridge, MA: NBER Macroeconomics Annual, MIT Press, 95–122.

IMF. (2010). *World economic outlook*, Chap. III. International Monetary Fund: Washington, DC.

Iron, J. S., & Bivens, J. (2010, July). Government debt and economic growth. *Economic Policy Institute Briefing Paper, 271*.

Kaminsky, G., & Reinhart, C. M. (1999). The twin crisis: The causes of banking and balance of payments problems. *American Economic Review, 89*(3), 473–500.

Krugman, P. (2010, October 21). British fashion victims. *The New York Times*.

Kumar, M., & Woo, J. (2010, July). *Public debt and growth* (IMF Working paper, WP/10/174).

Reinhart, C. M., & Reinhart, V. (2007, November 17). Is the US too big to fail? *VoxEU.org*.

Reinhart, C. M., & Reinhart, V. R. (2008). Is the U.S. too big to fail? *VoxEU*, May 2010.

Reinhart, C. M., & Rogoff, K. S. (2009). *This time is different: Eight centuries of financial folly.* Princeton, NJ: Princeton University Press.

Reinhart, C. M., & Rogoff, K. S. (2010a). *Growth in a time of debt. American Economic Review*, May (Revised from NBER working paper 15639, January 2010).

Reinhart, C. M., & Rogoff, K. S. (2010b). *From financial crash to debt crisis.* (NBER Working paper 15795, March). Forthcoming in *American Economic Review.*

Reinhart, C. M., Savastano, M. A., & Rogoff, K. S. (2003). Debt intolerance. In W. Brainard & G. Perry (Eds.), *Brookings papers on economic activity.* (An earlier version appeared as NBER Working paper 9908, August 2003).

Contemporary Arguments for Stimulus

A Brief Political and Economic History of Austerity

Original title: *The Austerity Delusion*
Published on *The Guardian* on April 29, 2015

In his rejoinder, Paul Krugman describes the distance between the realm of ideas and the realm of politics in the austerity debate. He notices that while austerian ideas have been defeated in the former, in some countries policies inspired by them are still dominant in the latter, and electorally successful for the feeling of economic responsibility wrongly associated to them. This is the case of the United Kingdom where, as opposed to the US, the ruling government and most of the media still support the austerity ideology. Through an inquiry into the history of austerity in its economic and political dimension, Krugman explains how we got to where we are.

By **Paul Krugman**

© The Author(s) 2017
R. Skidelsky and N. Fraccaroli, *Austerity vs Stimulus*,
DOI 10.1007/978-3-319-50439-1_4

In May 2010, as Britain headed into its last general election, elites all across the western world were gripped by austerity fever, a strange malady that combined extravagant fear with blithe optimism. Every country running significant budget deficits—as nearly all were in the aftermath of the financial crisis—was deemed at imminent risk of becoming another Greece unless it immediately began cutting spending and raising taxes. Concerns that imposing such austerity in already depressed economies would deepen their depression and delay recovery were airily dismissed; fiscal probity, we were assured, would inspire business-boosting confidence, and all would be well.

People holding these beliefs came to be widely known in economic circles as "austerians"—a term coined by the economist Rob Parenteau—and for a while the austerian ideology swept all before it.

But that was 5 years ago, and the fever has long since broken. Greece is now seen as it should have been seen from the beginning—as a unique case, with few lessons for the rest of us. It is impossible for countries such as the US and the UK, which borrow in their own currencies, to experience Greek-style crises, because they cannot run out of money—they can always print more. Even within the eurozone, borrowing costs plunged once the European Central Bank began to do its job and protect its clients against self-fulfilling panics by standing ready to buy government bonds if necessary. As I write this, Italy and Spain have no trouble raising cash—they can borrow at the lowest rates in their history, indeed considerably below those in Britain—and even Portugal's interest rates are within a whisker of those paid by HM Treasury.

All of the Economic Research that Allegedly Supported the Austerity Push Has Been Discredited

On the other side of the ledger, the benefits of improved confidence failed to make their promised appearance. Since the global turn to austerity in 2010, every country that introduced significant austerity has seen its economy suffer, with the depth of the suffering closely related to the harshness of the austerity. In late 2012, the IMF's chief economist, Olivier Blanchard, went so far as to issue what amounted to a mea culpa: although his organisation never bought into the notion that austerity would actually boost economic growth, the IMF now believes that it massively understated the damage that spending cuts inflict on a weak economy.

Meanwhile, all of the economic research that allegedly supported the austerity push has been discredited. Widely touted statistical results were, it turned out, based on highly dubious assumptions and procedures—plus a few outright mistakes—and evaporated under closer scrutiny.

It is rare, in the history of economic thought, for debates to get resolved this decisively. The austerian ideology that dominated elite discourse 5 years ago has collapsed, to the point where hardly anyone still believes it. Hardly anyone, that is, except the coalition that still rules Britain—and most of the British media.

I don't know how many Britons realise the extent to which their economic debate has diverged from the rest of the western world—the extent to which the UK seems stuck on obsessions that have been mainly laughed out of the discourse elsewhere. George Osborne and David Cameron boast that their policies saved Britain from a Greek-style crisis of soaring interest rates, apparently oblivious to the fact that interest rates are at historic lows all across the western world. The press seizes on Ed Miliband's failure to mention the budget deficit in a speech as a huge gaffe, a supposed revelation of irresponsibility; meanwhile, Hillary Clinton is talking, seriously, not about budget deficits but about the "fun deficit" facing America's children.

Is there some good reason why deficit obsession should still rule in Britain, even as it fades away everywhere else? No. This country is not different. The economics of austerity are the same—and the intellectual case as bankrupt—in Britain as everywhere else.

Stimulus and Its Enemies

When economic crisis struck the advanced economies in 2008, almost every government—even Germany—introduced some kind of stimulus programme, increasing spending and/or cutting taxes. There was no mystery why: it was all about zero. Normally, monetary authorities—the Federal Reserve, the Bank of England—can respond to a temporary economic downturn by cutting interest rates; this encourages private spending, especially on housing, and sets the stage for recovery. But there's a limit to how much they can do in that direction. Until recently, the conventional wisdom was that you couldn't cut interest rates below zero. We now know that this wasn't quite right, since many European bonds now pay slightly negative interest. Still, there can't be much room for sub-zero rates. And if cutting rates all the way to zero isn't enough to cure what ails the economy, the usual remedy for recession falls short.

So it was in 2008–2009. By late 2008 it was already clear in every major economy that conventional monetary policy, which involves pushing down the interest rate on short-term government debt, was going to be insufficient to fight the financial downdraft. Now what? The textbook answer was and is fiscal expansion: increase government spending both to create jobs directly and to put money in consumers' pockets; cut taxes to put more money in those pockets.

But won't this lead to budget deficits? Yes, and that's actually a good thing. An economy that is depressed even with zero interest rates is, in effect, an economy in which the public is trying to save more than businesses are willing to invest. In such an economy the government does everyone a service by running deficits and giving frustrated savers a chance to put their money to work. Nor does this borrowing compete with private investment. An economy where interest rates cannot go any lower is an economy awash in desired saving with no place to go, and deficit spending that expands the economy is, if anything, likely to lead to higher private investment than would otherwise materialise.

It's true that you can't run big budget deficits for ever (although you can do it for a long time), because at some point interest payments start to swallow too large a share of the budget. But it's foolish and destructive to worry about deficits when borrowing is very cheap and the funds you borrow would otherwise go to waste.

At some point you do want to reverse stimulus. But you don't want to do it too soon—specifically, you don't want to remove fiscal support as long as pedal-to-the-metal monetary policy is still insufficient. Instead, you want to wait until there can be a sort of handoff, in which the central bank offsets the effects of declining spending and rising taxes by keeping rates low. As John Maynard Keynes wrote in 1937: "The boom, not the slump, is the right time for austerity at the Treasury."

All of this is standard macroeconomics. I often encounter people on both the left and the right who imagine that austerity policies were what the textbook said you should do—that those of us who protested against the turn to austerity were staking out some kind of heterodox, radical position. But the truth is that mainstream, textbook economics not only justified the initial round of post-crisis stimulus, but said that this stimulus should continue until economies had recovered.

What we got instead, however, was a hard right turn in elite opinion, away from concerns about unemployment and toward a focus on slashing deficits, mainly with spending cuts. Why?

Conservatives like to Use the Alleged Dangers of Debt and Deficits as Clubs with Which to Beat the Welfare State and Justify Cuts in Benefits

Part of the answer is that politicians were catering to a public that doesn't understand the rationale for deficit spending, that tends to think of the government budget via analogies with family finances. When John Boehner, the Republican leader, opposed US stimulus plans on the grounds that "American families are tightening their belt, but they don't see government tightening its belt," economists cringed at the stupidity. But within a few months the very same line was showing up in Barack Obama's speeches, because his speechwriters found that it resonated with audiences. Similarly, the Labour party felt it necessary to dedicate the very first page of its 2015 general election manifesto to a "Budget Responsibility Lock", promising to "cut the deficit every year".

Let us not, however, be too harsh on the public. Many elite opinion-makers, including people who imagine themselves sophisticated on matters economic, demonstrated at best a higher level of incomprehension, not getting at all the logic of deficit spending in the face of excess desired saving. For example, in the spring of 2009 the Harvard historian and economic commentator Niall Ferguson, talking about the United States, was quite sure what would happen: "There is going to be, I predict, in the weeks and months ahead, a very painful tug-of-war between our monetary policy and our fiscal policy as the markets realise just what a vast quantity of bonds are going to have to be absorbed by the financial system this year. That will tend to drive the price of the bonds down, and drive up interest rates." The weeks and months turned into years—6 years, at this point—and interest rates remain at historic lows.

Beyond these economic misconceptions, there were political reasons why many influential players opposed fiscal stimulus even in the face of a deeply depressed economy. Conservatives like to use the alleged dangers of debt and deficits as clubs with which to beat the welfare state and justify cuts in benefits; suggestions that higher spending might actually be beneficial are definitely not welcome. Meanwhile, centrist politicians and pundits often try to demonstrate how serious and statesmanlike they are by calling for hard choices and sacrifice (by other people). Even Barack Obama's first inaugural address, given in the face of a plunging economy, largely consisted of hard-choices boilerplate. As a result, centrists were almost as uncomfortable with the notion of fiscal stimulus as the hard right.

In a way, the remarkable thing about economic policy in 2008–2009 was the fact that the case for fiscal stimulus made any headway at all against the forces of incomprehension and vested interests demanding harsher and harsher austerity. The best explanation of this temporary and limited success I've seen comes from the political scientist Henry Farrell, writing with the economist John Quiggin. Farrell and Quiggin note that Keynesian economists were intellectually prepared for the possibility of crisis, in a way that free-market fundamentalists weren't, and that they were also relatively media-savvy. So they got their take on the appropriate policy response out much more quickly than the other side, creating "the appearance of a new apparent consensus among expert economists" in favour of fiscal stimulus.

If this is right, there was inevitably going to be a growing backlash— a turn against stimulus and toward austerity—once the shock of the crisis wore off. Indeed, there were signs of such a backlash by the early fall of 2009. But the real turning point came at the end of that year, when Greece hit the wall. As a result, the year of Britain's last general election was also the year of austerity.

The Austerity Moment

From the beginning, there were plenty of people strongly inclined to oppose fiscal stimulus and demand austerity. But they had a problem: their dire warnings about the consequences of deficit spending kept not coming true. Some of them were quite open about their frustration with the refusal of markets to deliver the disasters they expected and wanted. Alan Greenspan, the former chairman of the Federal Reserve, in 2010: "Inflation and long-term interest rates, the typical symptoms of fiscal excess, have remained remarkably subdued. This is regrettable, because it is fostering a sense of complacency that can have dire consequences."

But he had an answer: "Growing analogies to Greece set the stage for a serious response." Greece was the disaster austerians were looking for. In September 2009 Greece's long-term borrowing costs were only 1.3% points higher than Germany's; by September 2010 that gap had increased sevenfold. Suddenly, austerians had a concrete demonstration of the dangers they had been warning about. A hard turn away from Keynesian policies could now be justified as an urgent defensive measure, lest your country abruptly turn into another Greece.

Still, what about the depressed state of western economies? The post-crisis recession bottomed out in the middle of 2009, and in most countries a recovery was under way, but output and employment were still far below normal. Wouldn't a turn to austerity threaten the still-fragile upturn?

Not according to many policymakers, who engaged in one of history's most remarkable displays of collective wishful thinking. Standard macroeconomics said that cutting spending in a depressed economy, with no room to offset these cuts by reducing interest rates that were already near zero, would indeed deepen the slump. But policymakers at the European Commission, the European Central Bank, and in the British government that took power in May 2010 eagerly seized on economic research that claimed to show the opposite.

The doctrine of "expansionary austerity" is largely associated with work by Alberto Alesina, an economist at Harvard. Alesina used statistical techniques that supposedly identified all large fiscal policy changes in advanced countries between 1970 and 2007, and claimed to find evidence that spending cuts, in particular, were often "associated with economic expansions rather than recessions". The reason, he and those who seized on his work suggested, was that spending cuts create confidence, and that the positive effects of this increase in confidence trump the direct negative effects of reduced spending.

Greece Was the Disaster Austerians Were Looking for

This may sound too good to be true—and it was. But policymakers knew what they wanted to hear, so it was, as Business Week put it, "Alesina's hour". The doctrine of expansionary austerity quickly became orthodoxy in much of Europe. "The idea that austerity measures could trigger stagnation is incorrect," declared Jean-Claude Trichet, then the president of the European Central Bank, because "confidence-inspiring policies will foster and not hamper economic recovery".

Besides, everybody knew that terrible things would happen if debt went above 90% of GDP.

Growth in a Time of Debt, the now-infamous 2010 paper by Carmen Reinhart and Kenneth Rogoff of Harvard University that claimed that 90% debt is a critical threshold, arguably played much less of a direct role in the turn to austerity than Alesina's work. After all, austerians didn't need Reinhart and Rogoff to provide dire scenarios about what could happen if deficits weren't reined in—they had the Greek crisis for that. At most, the Reinhart and Rogoff paper provided a backup bogeyman, an answer to those who kept pointing out that nothing like the Greek story seemed to be happening to countries that borrowed in their own currencies: even if interest rates were low, austerians could point to Reinhart and Rogoff and declare that high debt is very, very bad.

What Reinhart and Rogoff did bring to the austerity camp was academic cachet. Their 2009 book This Time is Different, which brought a vast array of historical data to bear on the subject of economic crises, was widely celebrated by both policymakers and economists—myself included—for its prescient warnings that we were at risk of a major crisis and that recovery from that crisis was likely to be slow. So they brought a lot of prestige to the austerity push when they were perceived as weighing in on that side of the policy debate. (They now claim that they did no such thing, but they did nothing to correct that impression at the time.)

When the coalition government came to power, then, all the pieces were in place for policymakers who were already inclined to push for austerity. Fiscal retrenchment could be presented as urgently needed to avert a Greek-style strike by bond buyers. "Greece stands as a warning of what happens to countries that lose their credibility, or whose governments pretend that difficult decisions can somehow be avoided," declared David Cameron soon after taking office. It could also be presented as urgently needed to stop debt, already almost 80% of GDP, from crossing the 90% red line. In a 2010 speech laying out his plan to eliminate the deficit, Osborne cited Reinhart and Rogoff by name, while declaring that "soaring government debt … is very likely to trigger the next crisis." Concerns about delaying recovery could be waved away with an appeal to positive effects on confidence. Economists who objected to any or all of these lines of argument were simply ignored.

But that was, as I said, 5 years ago.

Decline and Fall of the Austerity Cult

To understand what happened to austerianism, it helps to start with two charts.

The first chart (Fig. 1) shows interest rates on the bonds of a selection of advanced countries as of mid-April 2015. What you can see right away is that Greece remains unique, more than 5 years after it was heralded as an object lesson for all nations. Everyone else is paying very low interest rates by historical standards. This includes the United States, where the co-chairs of a debt commission created by President Obama confidently warned that crisis loomed within 2 years unless their recommendations were adopted; that was 4 years ago. It includes Spain and Italy, which faced a financial panic in 2011–2012, but saw that panic

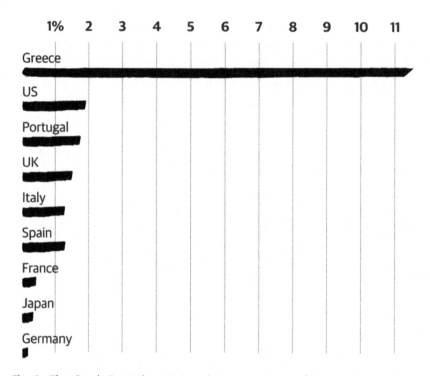

Fig. 1 The Greek Exception *10-year interest rates as of 14 April 2015. Source Bloomberg*

subside—despite debt that continued to rise—once the European Central Bank began doing its job as lender of last resort. It includes France, which many commentators singled out as the next domino to fall, yet can now borrow long-term for less than 0.5%. And it includes Japan, which has debt more than twice its gross domestic product yet pays even less.

Back in 2010 some economists argued that fears of a Greek-style funding crisis were vastly overblown—I referred to the myth of the "invisible bond vigilantes". Well, those bond vigilantes have stayed invisible. For countries such as the UK, the US, and Japan that borrow in their own currencies, it's hard to even see how the predicted crises could happen. Such countries cannot, after all, run out of money, and if worries about solvency weakened their currencies, this would actually help their economies in a time of weak growth and low inflation.

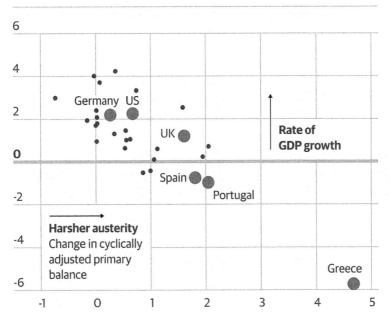

Fig. 2 Austerity and Growth 2009–2013 *more austere countries have a lower rate of GDP growth. Source* IMF

Figure 2 takes a bit more explaining. A couple of years after the great turn towards austerity, a number of economists realised that the austerians were performing what amounted to a great natural experiment. Historically, large cuts in government spending have usually occurred either in overheated economies suffering from inflation or in the aftermath of wars, as nations demobilise. Neither kind of episode offers much guidance on what to expect from the kind of spending cuts— imposed on already depressed economies—that the austerians were advocating. But after 2009, in a generalised economic depression, some countries chose (or were forced) to impose severe austerity, while others did not. So what happened?

In Fig. 2, each dot represents the experience of an advanced economy from 2009 to 2013, the last year of major spending cuts. The horizontal axis shows a widely used measure of austerity—the average annual change in the cyclically adjusted primary surplus, an estimate of what the difference between taxes and non-interest spending would be if the economy were at full employment. As you move further right on the graph, in other words, austerity becomes more severe. You can quibble with the details of this measure, but the basic result—harsh austerity in Ireland, Spain, and Portugal, incredibly harsh austerity in Greece—is surely right.

Meanwhile, the vertical axis shows the annual rate of economic growth over the same period. The negative correlation is, of course, strong and obvious—and not at all what the austerians had asserted would happen.

Again, some economists argued from the beginning that all the talk of expansionary austerity was foolish—back in 2010 I dubbed it belief in the "confidence fairy", a term that seems to have stuck. But why did the alleged statistical evidence—from Alesina, among others—that spending cuts were often good for growth prove so misleading?

The answer, it turned out, was that it wasn't very good statistical work. A review by the IMF found that the methods Alesina used in an attempt to identify examples of sharp austerity produced many misi-dentifications. For example, in 2000 Finland's budget deficit dropped sharply thanks to a stock market boom, which caused a surge in government revenue—but Alesina mistakenly identified this as a major auster-ity programme. When the IMF laboriously put together a new database of austerity measures derived from actual changes in spending and tax rates, it found that austerity has a consistently negative effect on growth.

Yet even the IMF's analysis fell short—as the institution itself eventu-ally acknowledged. I've already explained why: most historical episodes of austerity took place under conditions very different from those con-fronting western economies in 2010. For example, when Canada began a major fiscal retrenchment in the mid-1990s, interest rates were high, so the Bank of Canada could offset fiscal austerity with sharp rate cuts—not a useful model of the likely results of austerity in economies where inter-est rates were already very low. In 2010 and 2011, IMF projections of the effects of austerity programmes assumed that those effects would be simi-lar to the historical average. But a 2013 paper co-authored by the organi-sation's chief economist concluded that under post-crisis conditions the true effect had turned out to be nearly three times as large as expected.

So much, then, for invisible bond vigilantes and faith in the confi-dence fairy. What about the backup bogeyman, the Reinhart-Rogoff claim that there was a red line for debt at 90% of GDP?

Well, in early 2013 researchers at the University of Massachusetts examined the data behind the Reinhart-Rogoff work. They found that the results were partly driven by a spreadsheet error. More important, the results weren't at all robust: using standard statistical procedures rather than the rather odd approach Reinhart and Rogoff used, or adding a few more years of data, caused the 90% cliff to vanish. What was left was a modest negative correlation between debt and growth, and there was good reason to believe that in general slow growth causes high debt, not the other way around.

By about 2 years ago, then, the entire edifice of austerian economics had crumbled. Events had utterly failed to play out as the austerians predicted, while the academic research that allegedly supported the doctrine had withered under scrutiny. Hardly anyone has admitted being wrong—hardly anyone ever does, on any subject—but quite a few prominent austerians now deny having said what they did, in fact, say. The doctrine that ruled the world in 2010 has more or less vanished from the scene.

Except in Britain.

A Distinctly British Delusion

In the US, you no longer hear much from the deficit scolds who loomed so large in the national debate circa 2011. Some commentators and media organisations still try to make budget red ink an issue, but there's a pleading, even whining, tone to their exhortations. The day of the austerians has come and gone.

Yet Britain zigged just as the rest of us were zagging. By 2013, austerian doctrine was in ignominious retreat in most of the world—yet at that very moment much of the UK press was declaring that doctrine vindicated. "Osborne wins the battle on austerity," the Financial Times announced in September 2013, and the sentiment was widely echoed. What was going on? You might think that British debate took a different turn because the British experience was out of line with developments elsewhere—in particular, that Britain's return to economic growth in 2013 was somehow at odds with the predictions of standard economics. But you would be wrong.

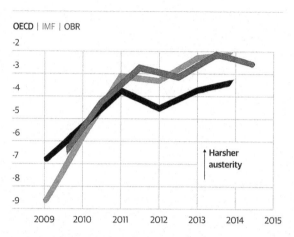

Fig. 3 Austerity in the UK *cyclically adjusted primary balance, percent of GDP.*
Source IMF, OECD, and OBR

The key point to understand about fiscal policy under Cameron and
Osborne is that British austerity, while very real and quite severe, was
mostly imposed during the coalition's first 2 years in power. Figure 3
shows estimates of our old friend the cyclically adjusted primary balance since 2009. I've included three sources—the IMF, the OECD, and
Britain's own Office of Budget Responsibility—just in case someone
wants to argue that any one of these sources is biased. In fact, every one
tells the same story: big spending cuts and a large tax rise between 2009
and 2011, not much change thereafter.

Given the fact that the coalition essentially stopped imposing new
austerity measures after its first 2 years, there's nothing at all surprising
about seeing a revival of economic growth in 2013.

Look back at Fig. 2, and specifically at what happened to countries
that did little if any fiscal tightening. For the most part, their economies
grew at between 2 and 4%. Well, Britain did almost no fiscal tightening in 2014, and grew 2.9%. In other words, it performed pretty much
exactly as you should have expected. And the growth of recent years
does nothing to change the fact that Britain paid a high price for the
austerity of 2010–2012.

British economists have no doubt about the economic damage wrought by austerity. The Centre for Macroeconomics in London regularly surveys a panel of leading UK economists on a variety of questions. When it asked whether the coalition's policies had promoted growth and employment, those disagreeing outnumbered those agreeing four to one. This isn't quite the level of unanimity on fiscal policy one finds in the US, where a similar survey of economists found only 2% disagreed with the proposition that the Obama stimulus led to higher output and employment than would have prevailed otherwise, but it's still an overwhelming consensus.

By this point, some readers will nonetheless be shaking their heads and declaring, "But the economy is booming, and you said that couldn't happen under austerity." But Keynesian logic says that a one-time tightening of fiscal policy will produce a one-time hit to the economy, not a permanent reduction in the growth rate. A return to growth after austerity has been put on hold is not at all surprising. As I pointed out recently: "If this counts as a policy success, why not try repeatedly hitting yourself in the face for a few minutes? After all, it will feel great when you stop."

In that case, however, what's with sophisticated media outlets such as the FT seeming to endorse this crude fallacy? Well, if you actually read that 2013 leader and many similar pieces, you discover that they are very carefully worded. The FT never said outright that the economic case for austerity had been vindicated. It only declared that Osborne had won the political battle, because the general public doesn't understand all this business about front-loaded policies, or for that matter the difference between levels and growth rates. One might have expected the press to seek to remedy such confusions, rather than amplify them. But apparently not.

Which brings me, finally, to the role of interests in distorting economic debate.

As Oxford's Simon Wren-Lewis noted, on the very same day that the Centre for Macroeconomics revealed that the great majority of British economists disagree with the proposition that austerity is good for growth, the Telegraph published on its front page a letter from 100 business leaders declaring the opposite. Why does big business love austerity and hate Keynesian economics? After all, you might expect corporate leaders to want policies that produce strong sales and hence strong profits.

I've already suggested one answer: scare talk about debt and deficits is often used as a cover for a very different agenda, namely an attempt to reduce the overall size of government and especially spending on social insurance. This has been transparently obvious in the United States, where many supposed deficit-reduction plans just happen to include sharp cuts in tax rates on corporations and the wealthy even as they take away healthcare and nutritional aid for the poor. But it's also a fairly obvious motivation in the UK, if not so crudely expressed. The "primary purpose" of austerity, the Telegraph admitted in 2013, "is to shrink the size of government spending"—or, as Cameron put it in a speech later that year, to make the state "leaner ... not just now, but permanently".

Beyond that lies a point made most strongly in the US by Mike Konczal of the Roosevelt Institute: business interests dislike Keynesian economics because it threatens their political bargaining power. Business leaders love the idea that the health of the economy depends on confidence, which in turn—or so they argue—requires making them happy. In the US there were, until the recent takeoff in job growth, many speeches and opinion pieces arguing that President Obama's anti-business rhetoric—which only existed in the right's imagination, but never mind—was holding back recovery. The message was clear: don't criticise big business, or the economy will suffer.

If the Political Opposition Won't Challenge the Coalition's Bad Economics, Who Will?

But this kind of argument loses its force if one acknowledges that job creation can be achieved through deliberate policy, that deficit spending, not buttering up business leaders, is the way to revive a depressed economy. So business interests are strongly inclined to reject standard macroeconomics and insist that boosting confidence—which is to say, keeping them happy—is the only way to go.

Still, all these motivations are the same in the United States as they are in Britain. Why are the US's austerians on the run, while Britain's still rule the debate?

It has been astonishing, from a US perspective, to witness the limpness of Labour's response to the austerity push. Britain's opposition has been amazingly willing to accept claims that budget deficits are the biggest economic issue facing the nation, and has made hardly any effort to challenge the extremely dubious proposition that fiscal policy under Blair and Brown was deeply irresponsible—or even the nonsensical proposition that this supposed fiscal irresponsibility caused the crisis of 2008–2009.

Why this weakness? In part it may reflect the fact that the crisis occurred on Labour's watch; American liberals should count themselves fortunate that Lehman Brothers didn't fall a year later, with Democrats holding the White House. More broadly, the whole European centre-left seems stuck in a kind of reflexive cringe, unable to stand up for its own ideas. In this respect Britain seems much closer to Europe than it is to America.

The closest parallel I can give from my side of the Atlantic is the erstwhile weakness of Democrats on foreign policy—their apparent inability back in 2003 or so to take a stand against obviously terrible ideas like the invasion of Iraq. If the political opposition won't challenge the coalition's bad economics, who will?

You might be tempted to say that this is all water under the bridge, given that the coalition, whatever it may claim, effectively called a halt to fiscal tightening midway through its term. But this story isn't over. Cameron is campaigning largely on a spurious claim to have "rescued" the British economy—and promising, if he stays in power, to continue making substantial cuts in the years ahead. Labour, sad to say, are echoing that position. So both major parties are in effect promising a new round of austerity that might well hold back a recovery that has, so far, come nowhere near to making up the ground lost during the recession and the initial phase of austerity.

For whatever the politics, the economics of austerity are no different in Britain from what they are in the rest of the advanced world. Harsh austerity in depressed economies isn't necessary, and does major damage when it is imposed. That was true of Britain 5 years ago—and it's still true today.

Stimulus, not Austerity Is the Key to Global Economic Recovery

Robert Skidelsky argues that a fiscal stimulus would be a more efficient policy to restore the economy. The credibility argument proposed by the austerians, in fact, does not hold, since commercial banks' confidence is too low for them to create the credit needed in the private sector. Moreover, from a political-economic perspective, a monetary stimulus (like the often-mentioned 'Quantitative Easing') in substitution to a fiscal one, is a highly conservative device, which does not allow the government to redirect investment according to its political (and therefore democratic) purposes, like reducing income inequality or promoting an economically-friendly demand.

By **Robert Skidelsky**

We all know how the global economic crisis began. The banks over-lent to the housing market. The subsequent burst of the housing bubble in the United States caused banks to fail, because banking had gone global and the big banks held one another's bad loans. Banking failure caused a credit crunch. Lending dried up and economies started shrinking.

So governments bailed out banks and economies, producing a sovereign debt crisis. With everyone busy deleveraging, economies failed to recover. Much of the world, especially Europe, but also the slightly less sickly US, remains stuck in a semi-slump.

So how do we escape from this hole? The familiar debate is between austerity and stimulus. "Austerians" believe that only balancing government budgets and shrinking national debts will restore investor confidence. The Keynesians believe that without a large fiscal stimulus—a deliberate temporary increase of the deficit—the European and US economies will remain stuck in recession for years to come.

I am one of those who believe that recovery from the crisis requires fiscal stimulus. I don't think monetary policy, even unorthodox monetary policy, can do the job. Confidence is too low for commercial banks to create credit on the scale needed to return to full employment and the pre-crisis growth trend, however many hundreds of billions of whatever cash central banks pour into them. We are learning all over again that the central bank cannot create whatever level of credit it wants.

Like Paul Krugman, Martin Wolf and others, I would expand fiscal deficits, not try to shrink them. I advocate this for the old-fashioned Keynesian reason that we are suffering from a deficiency of aggregate demand, that the multiplier is positive and that the most effective way to reduce the private and public debts a year or two down the line is by taking steps to boost growth in national income now.

But the argument between austerians and Keynesians over how to encourage sustained recovery intersects with another debate. Simply put, what kind of post-recovery economy do we want? This is where economics becomes political economy.

Those who believe that all was fine with the pre-crisis economy except for banks making crazy loans are convinced that preventing such crises in the future requires only banking reform. The new reform orthodoxy is "macro-prudential regulation" of commercial banks by the central bank. Some would go further and either nationalise the banks or break them up. But their horizon of reform is similarly confined to the banking sector, and they rarely ask what caused the banks to behave so badly.

In fact, it is possible to regard excessive bank lending as a symptom of deeper economic flaws. The economist Thomas Palley sees it as a means of offsetting growth in income inequality, with access to cheap credit replacing the broken welfare guarantee of social democracy. So reform requires redistribution of wealth and incomes.

Redistributive measures go quite well with stimulus policies, because they may be expected to increase aggregate demand in the short term (owing to lower-income households' higher propensity to consume) and minimise the economy's dependence on debt financing in the long term. Initial damage to the confidence of the business class caused by higher taxes on the wealthy would be balanced by the prospect of higher overall consumption.

Others argue that we should try to rebalance the economy not just from rich to poor, but also from energy-wasting to energy-saving. The premise of the green economic agenda is that we have reached the ecological limits of our current growth model, and that we will need to find ways of living that reduce demands on non-renewable sources of energy.

So stimulus policies should aim to stimulate not just demand per se. They must focus instead on stimulating ecologically-friendly demand. For example, greens advocate free municipal transport in major cities. In general, they argue, we need more care, not more cars, so stimulus money should go to health, education and environmental protection.

The truth is that any fiscally-driven recovery policy is bound to have reformist implications. That is why the austerians are so against it, and why even those who accept the theoretical case for a stimulus insist on implementing it through monetary policy alone.

Rebalancing the economy from gas-guzzling to energy-saving—and from private to public consumption—is bound to alter the goal of economic policy. Maximising GDP growth will no longer be the top priority; rather, it should be something we might want to call "happiness," or "wellbeing," or the "good life."

The radical case is that the pre-crisis economy crashed not because of preventable mistakes in banking, but because money had become the sole arbiter of value. So we should be energetic in seeking recovery, but not in a way that simply reproduces the structural flaws of the past.

As Dani Rodrik has well put it: "If economics were only about profit maximisation, it would be just another name for business administration. It is a social discipline, and society has other means of cost accounting beside market prices."

Part III

Confidence: The Object of the Debate

The previous part has shown—in an expository fashion—what are the arguments of both the two sides of the debate, and their roots in the thought of Keynes and Hayek. For one side (Alesina and the Bocconi scholars, Reinhart and Rogoff), austerity policies have a positive impact on growth; for the other side (represented by Krugman and Skidelsky) fiscal consolidation does the opposite, having a recessionary effect on growth, and therefore a fiscal stimulus is needed to revive the economy in times of crisis. Confidence clearly emerged as one of the main elements on which the two sides disagree. In this section, we will try to highlight what are the sources of this disagreement between contemporary economists.

Austerity: A Solution to Restore Markets' Confidence

Original Title: *The Austerity Question: 'How' is as important as 'How Much'*
In Corsetti, G. (2012) *Austerity: Too Much of a Good Thing?* VoxEu.

Alesina and Giavazzi explain the inverse relationship between public spending and growth during a recession. Reducing government's expenditure through austerity programs, their argument goes, restores confidence in the financial sector, which is therefore induced to invest, with a positive effect on growth. Such explanation leads the two scholars to remark that the size of austerity packages is not more important than the type of austerity program implemented by an economy: cutting spending is much better than raising taxes. In this distinction, confidence is a key explanatory variable in the theoretical framework of expansionary austerity: while tax-based stabilization lower investors' confidence, only budget cuts seem to be efficient in restoring it and bringing growth back.

By **Alberto Alesina** and **Francesco Giavazzi**

© The Author(s) 2017
R. Skidelsky and N. Fraccaroli, *Austerity vs Stimulus*,
DOI 10.1007/978-3-319-50439-1_5

Evidence on New Taxes Versus New Spending Cuts

Economists have engaged in some lively debates about how to measure and evaluate the effects of large fiscal adjustments episodes in OECD countries (Europe in particular). But a careful and fair reading of the evidence makes clear a few relatively uncontroversial points, despite the differences in approaches. The accumulated evidence from over 40 years of fiscal adjustments across the OECD speaks loud and clear:

1. First, adjustments achieved through spending cuts are less recessionary than those achieved through tax increases.
2. Second, spending-based consolidations accompanied by the right policies tend to be even less recessionary or even have a positive impact on growth.

These accompanying policies include easy money policy, liberalisation of goods and labour markets, and other structural reforms. There remains a lot of work to be done on identifying the appropriate accompanying policies and understanding the channels through which they help spending-based stabilisations, but the fact is there, as shown for instance in a recent paper by Roberto Perotti (2011). Third, only spending-based adjustments have eventually led to a permanent consolidation of the budget, as measured by the stabilisation (at least) if not the reduction of debts-to-GDP ratios.

IMF Research on the Austerity Composition Issue

Two recent IMF publications (IMF 2010, Chap. 3, and Devries et al. 2011) agree that spending-based adjustments are indeed those that work—but not because of their composition, rather because almost 'by chance' spending-based adjustments are accompanied by reductions in long-term interest rates, or a stabilisation of the exchange rate, the stock market, or all of the above. This line of argument is flawed on purely logical grounds. Financial prices—interest rates, the exchange rate, the stock market—are not exogenous. They respond to fiscal policy announcements. For instance, if investors perceive, correctly, that only spending-based adjustments will lead to a permanent consolidation of the budget, this will increase 'confidence' and result in lower interest rates and higher stock prices. A more convincing piece of evidence comes from a comparison of the effects of different 'types' of fiscal adjustment on confidence and on output. Tax-based stabilisations not only eventually fail, in the sense that they are unable to stop the growth of the debt-to-GDP ratio. When these fiscal packages are announced entrepreneurs' confidence falls sharply, and this is reflected in a fall in output. On the other hand, spending-based stabilisations (especially if accompanied by appropriate contemporaneous policies) do not negatively affect economic confidence contemporaneously. Moreover they are often accompanied by an increase in output within a year. It stands to reasons that European countries where tax revenues over GDP or close to 50% do not have the room to increase revenues even more. A paper by Harald Uhlig and Mathias Trabandt (2012) nicely shows how close many European countries are to the top of realistically measured Laffer curves. Thus any additional tax hikes would lead to relative low increases in tax revenues and could be very recessionary, through the usual supply- and demand-side channels. Given all of the above we should stop focusing fiscal policy discussions on the size of austerity programmes. A relatively small tax-based adjustment could be more recessionary than a larger one based upon spending cuts. Likewise, a small spending-based adjustment could be more effective at stabilising debt over GDP ratios than a larger tax-based one.

Digging Deeper into Austerity's Composition

One should go even further in disentangling the effects of composition.

- Which spending cuts are more likely to be effective?
- Which kind of tax reforms could achieve the same amount of tax revenue with fewer distortions?

- From where should market liberalisations start, and how fast should they proceed? Some answers may be the same for all countries, others may differ.

For instance, in general moving taxation towards the VAT and away from income taxes is preferable. In some countries there is no way out without a substantial raise in retirement age and cuts in government employment. Incidentally this provides a clear link with labour-market reforms. Public-sector employment can only be reduced after firing constraints are moved and appropriate safety nets are put in place. Similarly the emphasis on the need and productivity of physical infrastructures is often misleading, at least in many countries.

Conclusion

Until this critical principle—'how' is as important as 'how much'—is embraced, the austerity debate in Europe will continue to be completely out of whack with real economic consequences. We are in for a big disappointment on the centrepiece of Eurozone austerity—the Fiscal Compact. The Fiscal Compact bears the seeds of its failure:

- The new Fiscal Compact that Europe has decided to impose upon itself through a treaty change makes no mention of the composition of fiscal packages.
- European economies will remain stagnant—if not further fall into recession—if adjustments will be made mostly on the tax side and debt ratios will not come down.
- And in the end, as was the case with the Growth and Stability Pact, the rules will be abandoned.

References

Devries, P., Guajardo, J., Leigh, D., & Pescatori, A. (2011). *A new action-based dataset of fiscal consolidation* (IMF Working Paper No. 11/128).

IMF. (2010). *"Chapter 3", World economic outlook.* Washington, DC: International Monetary Fund.

Perotti, R. (2011). *The 'Austerity Myth': Gain without pain?* (NBER Working Paper No. 17571).

Trabandt, M., & Uhlig, H. (2012). *How do Laffer curves differ across countries* (NBER Working Paper No. 17862).

Myths of Austerity

In the following article, Krugman explains the austerians' view through a stylised framework in which investors—that he calls "Bond vigilantes"— evaluate a government's fiscal policy looking at its debt's dynamic. According to austerity-supporters, governments are hostages of bond vigilantes, who can promptly react to any stimulus policy by "pulling the plug" through speculative attacks. Reducing the debt would instead make the bond holders more confident and consequently safeguard governments from their speculative attacks, allowing therefore a smooth economic recovery (on this mechanism lies the "expansionary effect" of fiscal contraction). Krugman, though, does not share this view, since the evidence on which this theory is based is shattered and often ambiguous. The confidence brought by austerity is therefore as imaginary as a "myth", and for the same reason the Nobel prize names it "confidence fairy".

by **Paul Krugman**

When I was young and naïve, I believed that important people took positions based on careful consideration of the options. Now I know better. Much of what Serious People believe rests on prejudices, not analysis.

© The Author(s) 2017
R. Skidelsky and N. Fraccaroli, *Austerity vs Stimulus*,
DOI 10.1007/978-3-319-50439-1_6

And these prejudices are subject to fads and fashions. Which brings me to the subject [of this article]. For the last few months, I and others have watched, with amazement and horror, the emergence of a consensus in policy circles in favor of immediate fiscal austerity. That is, somehow it has become conventional wisdom that now is the time to slash spending, despite the fact that the world's major economies remain deeply depressed.

This conventional wisdom isn't based on either evidence or careful analysis. Instead, it rests on what we might charitably call sheer speculation, and less charitably call figments of the policy elite's imagination—specifically, on belief in what I've come to think of as the invisible bond vigilante and the confidence fairy.

Bond vigilantes are investors who pull the plug on governments they perceive as unable or unwilling to pay their debts. Now there's no question that countries can suffer crises of confidence (see Greece, debt of). But what the advocates of austerity claim is that (a) the bond vigilantes are about to attack America, and (b) spending anything more on stimulus will set them off.

What reason do we have to believe that any of this is true? Yes, America has long-run budget problems, but what we do on stimulus over the next couple of years has almost no bearing on our ability to deal with these long-run problems. As Douglas Elmendorf, the director of the Congressional Budget Office, recently put it, "There is no intrinsic contradiction between providing additional fiscal stimulus today, while the unemployment rate is high and many factories and offices are underused, and imposing fiscal restraint several years from now, when output and employment will probably be close to their potential."

Nonetheless, every few months we're told that the bond vigilantes have arrived, and we must impose austerity now now now to appease them. Three months ago, a slight uptick in long-term interest rates was greeted with near hysteria: "Debt Fears Send Rates Up," was the headline at The Wall Street Journal, although there was no actual evidence of such fears, and Alan Greenspan pronounced the rise a "canary in the mine."

Since then, long-term rates have plunged again. Far from fleeing U.S. government debt, investors evidently see it as their safest bet in a stumbling economy. Yet the advocates of austerity still assure us that bond vigilantes will attack any day now if we don't slash spending immediately.

But don't worry: spending cuts may hurt, but the confidence fairy will take away the pain. "The idea that austerity measures could trigger stagnation is incorrect," declared Jean-Claude Trichet, the president of the European Central Bank, in a recent interview. Why? Because "confidence-inspiring policies will foster and not hamper economic recovery."

What's the evidence for the belief that fiscal contraction is actually expansionary, because it improves confidence? (By the way, this is precisely the doctrine expounded by Herbert Hoover in 1932.) Well, there have been historical cases of spending cuts and tax increases followed by economic growth. But as far as I can tell, every one of those examples proves, on closer examination, to be a case in which the negative effects of austerity were offset by other factors, factors not likely to be relevant today. For example, Ireland's era of austerity-with-growth in the 1980s depended on a drastic move from trade deficit to trade surplus, which isn't a strategy everyone can pursue at the same time.

And current examples of austerity are anything but encouraging. Ireland has been a good soldier in this crisis, grimly implementing savage spending cuts. Its reward has been a Depression-level slump—and financial markets continue to treat it as a serious default risk. Other good soldiers, like Latvia and Estonia, have done even worse—and all three nations have, believe it or not, had worse slumps in output and employment than Iceland, which was forced by the sheer scale of its financial crisis to adopt less orthodox policies.

So the next time you hear serious-sounding people explaining the need for fiscal austerity, try to parse their argument. Almost surely, you'll discover that what sounds like hardheaded realism actually rests on a foundation of fantasy, on the belief that invisible vigilantes will punish us if we're bad and the confidence fairy will reward us if we're good. And real-world policy—policy that will blight the lives of millions of working families—is being built on that foundation.

Debating the Confidence Fairy

Skidelsky further considers the confidence-argument. Advocates of austerity, like Alesina and Rogoff, argue that cutting public spending has a positive effect on growth as it restores confidence in the investors. In other words, the focus should not be on the impact of austerity on growth, but on expectations: "the belief [not the fact] that it would work—the confidence fairy—would ensure its success." For stimulus-advocates, like Skidelsky and Krugman, this explanation cannot hold: inserting the confidence argument "between the cause and effect of a policy does not change the logic of the policy," that it will still have negative effects on growth. It is for the lack of foundations of this discourse that some stimulus-supporters, like Krugman, named this argument "confidence fairy."

By **Robert Skidelsky**

In 2011, the Nobel laureate economist Paul Krugman characterized conservative discourse on budget deficits in terms of "bond vigilantes" and the "confidence fairy." Unless governments cut their deficits, the bond vigilantes will put the screws to them by forcing up interest rates.

© The Author(s) 2017
R. Skidelsky and N. Fraccaroli, *Austerity vs Stimulus*,
DOI 10.1007/978-3-319-50439-1_7

But if they do cut, the confidence fairy will reward them by stimulating private spending more than the cuts depress it.

Krugman thought the "bond vigilante" claim might be valid for a few countries, such as Greece, but argued that the "confidence fairy" was no less imaginary than the one that collects children's teeth. Cutting a deficit in a slump could never cause a recovery. Political rhetoric can stop a good policy from being adopted, but it cannot stop it from succeeding. Above all, it cannot make a bad policy work.

I recently debated this point with Krugman at a *New York Review of Books* event. My argument was that adverse expectations could affect a policy's results, not just the chances that it will be adopted. For example, if people thought that government borrowing was simply deferred taxation, they might save more to meet their expected future tax bill.

On reflection, I think I was wrong. The confidence factor affects government decision-making, but it does not affect the results of decisions. Except in extreme cases, confidence cannot cause a bad policy to have good results, and a lack of it cannot cause a good policy to have bad results, any more than jumping out of a window in the mistaken belief that humans can fly can offset the effect of gravity.

The sequence of events in the Great Recession that began in 2008 bears this out. At first, governments threw everything at it. This prevented the Great Recession from becoming Great Depression II. But, before the economy reached bottom, the stimulus was turned off, and austerity—accelerated liquidation of budget deficits, mainly by cuts in spending—became the order of the day.

Once winded political elites had recovered their breath, they began telling a story designed to preclude any further fiscal stimulus. The slump had been created by fiscal extravagance, they insisted, and therefore could be cured only by fiscal austerity. And not any old austerity: it was spending on the poor, not the rich, that had to be cut, because such spending was the real cause of the trouble.

Any Keynesian knows that cutting the deficit in a slump is bad policy. A slump, after all, is defined by a deficiency in total spending. To try to cure it by spending less is like trying to cure a sick person by bleeding.

So it was natural to ask economist/advocates of bleeding like Harvard's Alberto Alesina and Kenneth Rogoff how they expected their cure to work. Their answer was that the belief that it would work—the confidence fairy—would ensure its success.

More precisely, Alesina argued that while bleeding on its own would worsen the patient's condition, its beneficial impact on expectations would more than offset its debilitating effects. Buoyed by assurance of recovery, the half-dead patient would leap out of bed, start running, jumping, and eating normally, and would soon be restored to full vigor. The bleeding school produced some flaky evidence to show that this had happened in a few instances.

Conservatives who wanted to cut public spending for ideological reasons found the bond vigilante/confidence fairy story to be ideally suited to their purpose. Talking up previous fiscal extravagance made a bond-market attack on heavily indebted governments seem more plausible (and more likely); the confidence fairy promised to reward fiscal frugality by making the economy more productive.

With the help of professors like Alesina, conservative conviction could be turned into scientific prediction. And when Alesina's cure failed to produce rapid recovery, there was an obvious excuse: it had not been applied with enough vigor to be "credible."

The cure, such as it was, finally came about, years behind schedule, not through fiscal bleeding, but by massive monetary stimulus. When the groggy patient eventually staggered to its feet, the champions of fiscal bleeding triumphantly proclaimed that austerity had worked.

The moral of the tale is simple: Austerity in a slump does not work, for the reason that the medieval cure of bleeding a patient never worked: it enfeebles instead of strengthening. Inserting the confidence fairy between the cause and effect of a policy does not change the logic of the policy; it simply obscures the logic for a time. Recovery may come about despite fiscal austerity, but never because of it.

Although Krugman invented his discourse for an American readership, it perfectly fits the British case as well. In his first budget in June 2010, Chancellor of the Exchequer George Osborne warned that "you can see in Greece an example of a country that didn't face up to its problems, and that's a fate I am determined to avoid."

In presenting the United Kingdom's 2015 budget in March, Osborne claimed that austerity had made Britain "walk tall" again. On May 7, that claim will be put to the test in the UK's parliamentary election. British voters, still wobbly from Osborne's medicine, can be forgiven if they decide that they should have stayed in bed.

Confidence in the UK Is Different from the One in the Eurozone

Original title: 'Managing a fragile Eurozone'.
Published on *VoxEU* on May 10, 2011.

British austerians often argue that if the UK was to run budget deficit, it would risk ending up like Greece, or other European countries (Spain, Italy, Ireland, Portugal) that after the crash experienced a steep rise of the interest rates on their bond together with an increase in the unemployment rates. This analogy is used, for example, by Vince Cable to defend the restrictive fiscal policies of the Conservative-Liberal coalition, in an article contained in the following section of this book.

In the analysis that follows, prof. Paul De Grauwe (LSE) shows how fiscal policies have different effects on confidence in the UK compared to the other Eurozone countries, like Greece or Spain. As the Belgian economist observes, although Spain has a smaller debt-to-GDP than Great Britain, it experienced a significantly higher and faster hike of interest rates than the UK after the crisis, signalling that the confidence of investors steeply declined in the former despite the higher debt of the latter. While putting these two graphs is sufficient to debunk the analogy with Greece, it remains still left to explain why confidence is stronger in the UK than in the Eurozone

© The Author(s) 2017
R. Skidelsky and N. Fraccaroli, *Austerity vs Stimulus*,
DOI 10.1007/978-3-319-50439-1_8

countries. According to De Grauwe, the reason lies on the fragile design of the European Monetary Union.

By **Paul De Grauwe**

Why does the Spanish government pay significantly more to borrow than the UK government—despite having a smaller deficit and lower overall debt? This column argues that the reason lies in the Eurozone's fragility. Its members lose their ability to issue debt in a currency over which they have full control. The column discusses ways to deal with this weakness.

A monetary union is more than just a single currency and a single central bank. Countries that join a monetary union lose more than one instrument of economic policy. They lose their capacity to issue debt in a currency over which they have full control.

This separation of decisions—debt issuance on the one hand and monetary control on the other—creates a critical vulnerability; a loss of market confidence can unleash a self-fulfilling spiral that drives the country into default (see Kopf 2011). The economic logic of this is straightforward.

Suppose that investors begin to fear a default by, say, Spain. They sell Spanish government bonds and this raises the interest rate. If this goes far enough, the Spanish government will experience a liquidity crisis, i.e. it cannot obtain funds to roll over its debt at reasonable interest rates. The Spanish government cannot force the Bank of Spain to buy government debt and although the ECB could provide all the liquidity in the world, the Spanish government does not control that institution. This can be self-fulfilling since if investors think that the Spanish government might reach this end point, they'll sell Spanish bonds in a way that turns their fears into a reality.

It doesn't work like this for countries capable of issuing debt in their own currency. To see this, re-run the Spanish example for the UK. If investors began to fear that the UK government might default on its debt, they would sell their UK government bonds and this would drive up the interest rate.

After selling these bonds, these investors would have pounds that most probably they would want to get rid of by selling them in the foreign-exchange market. The price of the pound would drop until somebody else would be willing to buy these pounds. The effect of this

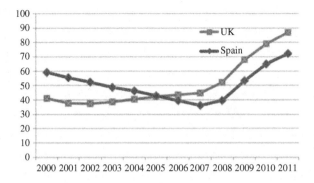

Fig. 1 Gross government debt (% of GDP)—Spain and UK (2000–2011). *Source* AMECO

mechanism is that the pounds would remain bottled up in the UK money market to be invested in UK assets.

Put differently, the UK money stock would remain unchanged. Part of that stock of money would probably be re-invested in UK government securities. But even if that were not the case so that the UK government cannot find the funds to roll over its debt at reasonable interest rates, it would certainly force the Bank of England to buy up the government securities. Thus the UK government is ensured that the liquidity is around to fund its debt. This means that investors cannot precipitate a liquidity crisis in the UK that could force the UK government into default. There is a superior force of last resort, the Bank of England.

This different mechanism explains why the Spanish government now pays 200 basis points more on its 10-year bonds than the UK government despite the fact that its debt and deficit are significantly lower than the UK ones. This contrast is shown vividly in Figs. 1 and 2.

Because of the liquidity flows triggered by changing market sentiments, member countries of a monetary union become vulnerable to these market sentiments. These can lead to "sudden stops" in the funding of the government debt (Calvo 1988), setting in motion a devilish interaction between liquidity and solvency crises. For the liquidity crisis raises the interest rate which in turn leads to a solvency crisis. This problem is not unique for members of a monetary union. It has been found to be very important in emerging economies that cannot issue debt in

Fig. 2 Ten-year government bond rates—Spain and UK (2009–2010). *Source* Datastream

their own currencies. (See Eichengreen et al. 2005 who have analysed these problems in great detail).

There are important further implications of the increased vulnerability of member-countries of a monetary union. (In De Grauwe 2011 these implications are developed in greater detail; see also Wolf 2011). One of these is that members of a monetary union loose much of their capacity to apply counter-cyclical budgetary policies. When during a recession the budget deficits increase, this risks creating a loss of confidence of investors in the capacity of the sovereign to service the debt. This has the effect of raising the interest rate, making the recession worse, and leading to even higher budget deficits. As a result, countries in a monetary union can be forced into a bad equilibrium, characterised by deflation, high interest rates, high budget deficits and a banking crisis (see De Grauwe 2011 for a more formal analysis).

These systemic features of a monetary union have not sufficiently been taken into account in the new design of the economic governance of the Eurozone. Too much of this new design has been influenced by the notion (based on moral hazard thinking) that when a country experiences budget deficits and increasing debts, it should be punished by high interest rates and tough austerity programmes. This approach is usually not helpful in restoring budgetary balance.

In addition, a number of features of the design of financial assistance in the Eurozone as embodied in the European Stability Mechanism will have the effect of making countries even more sensitive to shifting market sentiments. In particular, the "collective action clauses" which will be imposed on the future issue of government debt in the Eurozone, will increase the nervousness of financial markets. With each recession government bondholders, fearing haircuts, will "run for cover", i.e. selling government bonds, thereby making a default crisis more likely. All this is likely to increase the risk that countries in the Eurozone lose their capacity to let the automatic stabilisers in the budget play their necessary role of stabilising the economy.

A monetary union creates collective problems. When one government faces a debt crisis this is likely to lead to major financial repercussions in other member countries (see Arezki et al. 2011 for evidence). This is so because a monetary union leads to intense financial integration. The externalities inherent in a monetary union lead to the need for collective action, in the form of a European Monetary Fund (Gros and Mayer 2010). This idea has been implemented when the European Financial Stability Facility was instituted (which will obtain a permanent character in 2013 when it is transformed into the European Stability Mechanism). Surely, when providing mutual financial assistance, it is important to create the right incentives for governments so as to avoid moral hazard. Discipline by the threat of punishment is part of such an incentive scheme. However, too much importance has been given to punishment and not enough to assistance in the new design of financial assistance in the Eurozone.

This excessive emphasis on punishment is also responsible for a refusal to introduce new institutions that will protect member countries from the vagaries of financial markets that can trap countries into a debt crisis and a bad equilibrium. One such an institution is the collective issue of government bonds (for recent proposals see Delpla and von Weizsäcker 2010; De Grauwe and Moesen 2009; Juncker and Tremonti 2010). Such a common bond issue makes it possible to solve the coordination failure that arises when markets in a self-fulfilling way guide countries to a bad equilibrium. It is equivalent to setting up a collective defence system against the vagaries of euphoria and fears that regularly grip financial markets, and have the effect of leading to centrifugal forces in a monetary union.

A monetary union can only function if there is a collective mechanism of mutual support and control. Such a collective mechanism exists in a political union. In the absence of a political union, the member countries of the Eurozone are condemned to fill in the necessary pieces of such a collective mechanism. The debt crisis has made it possible to fill in a few of these pieces. What has been achieved, however, is still far from sufficient to guarantee the survival of the Eurozone.

References

Arezki, R., Candelon, B., & Sy, A. (2011, March). *Sovereign rating news and financial markets spillovers: Evidence from the European debt crisis.* (IMF Working Paper (11/69)).

Calvo, G. (1988). Servicing the public debt: The role of expectations. *American Economic Review, 78*(4), 647–661.

De Grauwe, P., & Moesen, W. (2009, May/June). Gains for all: A proposal for a common eurobond. *Intereconomics.*

De Grauwe, P. (2011, May). *The governance of a fragile eurozone. CEPS Working Document* (N. 346).

Delpla, J., & von Weizsäcker, J. (2010, May). The Blue Bond Proposal. *Bruegel Policy Brief,* Bruegel. http://bruegel.org/2010/05/the-blue-bond-proposal/.

Eichengreen, B., Hausmann, R., & Panizza U. (2005). The pain of original sin. In B. Eichengreen, & R. Hausmann (Eds.), *Other people's money: Debt denomination and financial instability in emerging market economies.* Chicago: Chicago University Press.

Gros, D., & Mayer T. (2010, May 17). Towards a European monetary fund. *CEPS Policy Brief,* Centre for European Policy Studies. https://www.ceps.eu/publications/towards-european-monetary-fund.

Juncker, J.-C., & Tremonti G. (2010, December 5). E-bonds would end the crisis. *The Financial Times.*

Kopf, C. (2011, March 15). Restoring financial stability in the euro area. *CEPS Policy Briefs,* Centre for European Policy Studies. https://www.ceps.eu/publications/restoring-financial-stability-euro-area.

Wolf, M. (2011, May 4). Managing the eurozone's fragility. *The Financial Times.*

Confidence Beyond Debt: The Role of Monetary Policy

Original title: *QE in the Eurozone has failed.*
Published on *Pieria* on November 18, 2015.

De Grauwe's article showed how important the coordination of monetary and fiscal policy is to cope with crises. Delegating monetary policy to a higher-tier independent authority, the ECB, while keeping fiscal policy in the hands of Member states governments, makes this coordination harder in the Eurozone. For austerity-supporters, though, this is not a big problem: once we guarantee restrictive fiscal policies (as it is done in Europe with the establishment of the Maastricht thresholds on debt and deficit), expansionary monetary policies like the Quantitative Easing are enough to restore confidence in the financial markets. Such theory, though, is not supported by the recent economic data illustrated in this article by Thomas Fazi, who assesses the failure of the European QE. To be effective, the monetary stimulus should not act alone, but it should be instead coordinated with an expansionary fiscal policy. This solution, though, cannot be implemented in the current institutional setting of the Eurozone, which keeps the fiscal side at a national level and strictly separated from the monetary one.

By **Thomas Fazi**

© The Author(s) 2017
R. Skidelsky and N. Fraccaroli, *Austerity vs Stimulus*,
DOI 10.1007/978-3-319-50439-1_9

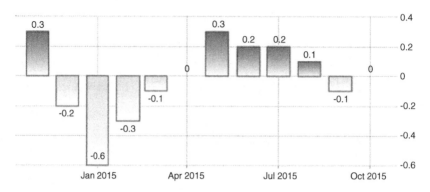

Fig. 1 EU inflation rate (Jan. 2015–Oct. 2015). *Source* Tradingeconomics.com. Data: Eurostat

Eight months have passed since the ECB started its own quantitative easing (QE) program, and almost everyone in Europe seems to agree with Mario Draghi that 'QE has been a success'. But is such enthusiasm warranted? Let's take a look at the data. The obvious starting place is the inflation rate. As is well known, the ECB's mandate only foresees a single measurable objective—maintaining the inflation rate 'below, but close to, 2 per cent'—and it is thus logical to judge the central bank's actions first and foremost according to this parameter (as narrow as it may be), especially since one of the stated aims of the ECB's QE program is to bring the inflation rate back towards the 2% target.

So how did the program fare in this respect? Not well: in September the inflation rate turned negative again (−0.1%—coincidentally, the exact same level registered in March of this year, when the ECB launched its asset-buying program) (Fig. 1).

Focusing on whether the inflation rate is just above or below 0% is beyond the point, though: the fact of the matter is that the euro area's average inflation rate—notwithstanding the huge inflation differentials between countries—has been below the ECB's target of 2% since late 2012, and below 1.5%—which essentially amounts to deflation, according to a generally accepted guideline—since the beginning of 2013. That is, for almost three consecutive years (Fig. 2).

If we look the GDP growth rate for the euro area, the conclusions are even more damning: as one can see in the following image, the growth rate actually starts to contract once again—putting an end to the slow

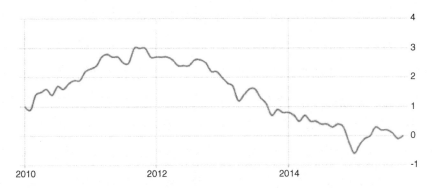

Fig. 2 EU inflation rate. *Source* Tradingeconomics.com. Data: Eurostat

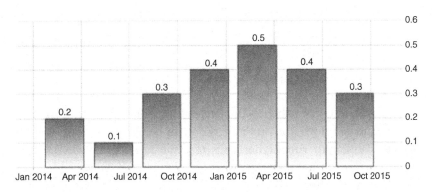

Fig. 3 EU GDP growth rate (Jan. 2014–Oct. 2015). *Source* Tradingeconomics. com. Data: Eurostat

climb commenced in 2014—precisely a few months after the launch of the QE program, in March 2015 (Fig. 3).

Interestingly, many people credit QE for lowering government bond yields across the eurozone, but periphery bond yields have been steadily declining since 2012, with QE having almost no effect whatsoever on the general trend. The Italian-German bond spread provides a good case in point (Fig. 4).

These numbers would be sufficient to dismiss the ECB's QE program as a catastrophic failure and to call for a radical change of course. But let's try to understand why European-style QE has failed so miserably. The main cause is without the doubt the continued, absurd and

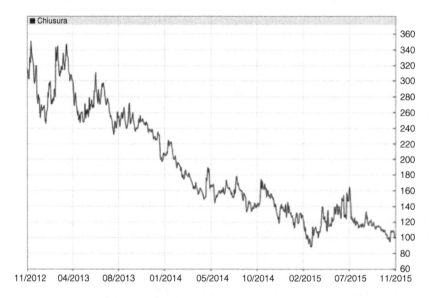

Fig. 4 BTP BUND 1080 days (Nov 15, 2015—weekly chart). *Source* Borse.it

unjustifiable refusal on behalf of national and European authorities to take advantage on what is probably the main benefit of quantitative easing—the ability to run higher deficits while keeping borrowing costs down—to pursue a fiscal expansion, as the United States did in the aftermath of the financial crisis (and as advocated by growing number of mainstream economists and commentators).

What this means is that, when speaking of QE, it's important to differentiate between QE as a purely monetary tool and QE as a monetary-fiscal tool: i.e., an expansionary monetary policy meant to facilitate an expansionary fiscal policy. The two are radically different. Unfortunately, European QE falls squarely in the first category: in other words, Draghi and the other members of European/national establishments continue to base their policy decisions on the assumption that monetary loosening is capable in itself—i.e., without the need for fiscal operations—of stimulating the economy, by easing credit conditions (thus boosting lending) and by depreciating the currency (thus boosting exports). The numbers tell a different story, though.

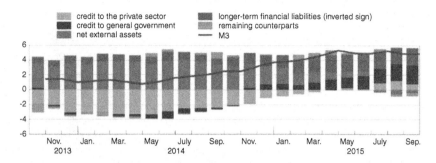

Fig. 5 Contribution of the M3 counterparts to the annual growth rate of M3 (percentage points)

Let's take bank lending. Even though bank lending in the eurozone is slowly increasing—and even accepting the dubious premise that economic recovery is dependent on increased lending, it is still well below the level that would be needed. As one can see in the following figure, taken from a recent ECB report, the lion's share of the growth in the money supply (M3) over the past year and a half is accounted for by an increase in credit to the public sector—explaining the continued rise in the euro area's government debt, not to the private sector (Fig. 5).

According to a recent survey by Commerzbank, quantitative easing has had almost no effect on bank lending: on balance, roughly 85% of the banks said that QE has not increased lending and practically no bank saw a 'considerable' effect of QE. As the report states, 'liquidity is obviously no key factor that limits lending' (Fig. 6).

This confirms what post-Keynesian theory has always advocated: banks do not 'lend out' reserves (or deposits, for that matter). The causality actually works in reverse: when a bank makes a new loan, it simply taps some numbers into a computer and creates brand new money 'out of thin air', which it then deposits into the borrower's account. Only then, if it has insufficient reserves, does the bank turn to the central bank, which is obliged to provide reserves on demand. Pre-existing deposits aren't even touched—or needed, for that matter. In short, the money supply, not unlike the rest of the economy, is endogenously demand-driven. This is why in the face of weak demand, where the

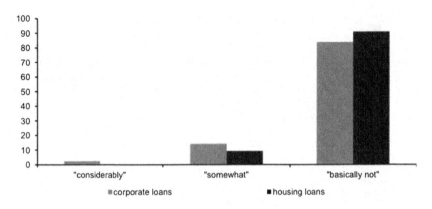

Fig. 6 Eurozone—QE liquidity rarely used for lending "Over the past six months, has your bank used the additional liquidity arising from the ECB's asset purchase programme for granting loans to non-financial corporations and households?" (in percent). *Source* ECB Bank Lending Survey, Commerzbank Research

economic and profitability prospects offered by the real economy are dim—not to mention in a deflationary-recessionary context such as the one that the eurozone finds itself it, in which balance sheets are being repaired, household and business demand for credit is weak, corporate insolvencies are on the rise and credit intermediation channels are impaired, credit dries up, regardless of the amount of QE that a central bank engages in. This is known as a 'credit trap'.

This is compounded by the fact that average euro area interest rates for companies and households are still relatively high—just above 2%, in the face of very low or even negative inflation rates in a number of countries—despite ECB interest rates being at a historical low (Fig. 7).

Both symptom and cause of the overall low level of lending—and the depressed state of the European economy in general—is the dizzying and rapidly-growing volume of non-performing loans (NPLs) across the continent. According to a recent study published on VoxEU.org, for the EU as a whole, NPLs stood at over 9% of GDP at the end of 2014—equivalent to a staggering 1.2 trillion euros, more than double the level in 2009. NPLs are particularly elevated in some southern countries, such as Italy, Greece, Portugal and Cyprus. And they are generally

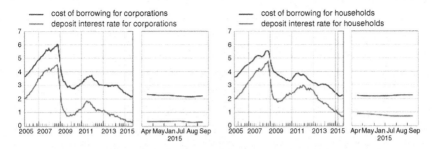

Fig. 7 Bank interest rates on new loans to, and deposits from, euro area corporations and households (percentages per annum)

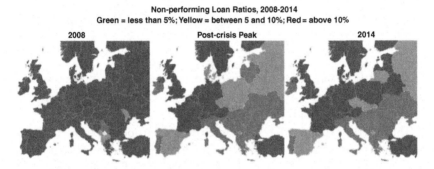

Fig. 8 Non-performing loan ratios after the global crisis in Europe (2008–2014). *Note* FSIs are computed using consolidated bank data and therefore do not reflect only domestic NPLs. *Source* IMF Financial Sector Indicators (FSIs) and countries authorities

concentrated in the corporate sector, most notably among small and medium-sized enterprises (SMEs), which contribute almost two-thirds of Europe's output and employment, and tend to be more reliant on bank financing than large firms (Fig. 8).

This has worrying implications not only for the financial stability of the euro area but also for the prospects of economic recovery, given that 'higher NPLs tend to reduce the credit-to-GDP ratio and GDP growth, while increasing unemployment', the study states. This is a direct result of the austerity policies pursued in recent years, which have exacerbated the recession in a number of countries, further deteriorating the balance sheets of families and corporates and, in turn, those of banks. QE can

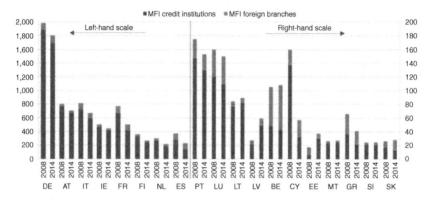

Fig. 9 Number of credit institutions and foreign branches in 2008 and 2014. *Note* Figures for Latvia include credit unions starting from 2013. *Source* ECB MFI statistics

do very little to stem this dramatic trend (and according to some studies it might actually have worsened it, by negatively impacting the profitability of banks through the lowering of interest rates).

This partly explains the silent die-off of European banks that has been underway since 2008. In its recent Report on financial structures, the ECB notes that in 2014 the total number of credit institutions decreased further to 5614, down from 6054 in 2013 and 6774 in 2008. In other words, more than 1000 credit institutions have disappeared or, more likely, have been gobbled up since the start of the crisis (Fig. 9).

This means that we are in the presence of a financial system that is at once more concentrated and consolidated (and thus increasingly 'too big to fail') but also more fragile, and as a result less likely to support the real economy in any meaningful way. In such a context, hoping to 'encourage' banks to lend through quantitative easing is, at best, delusional.

And what about the second channel through which QE is supposed to stimulate the economy, the boosting of exports through a further depreciation of the euro? The eurozone is already running a current account surplus of 3.7% of GDP, the largest in the world in nominal terms. A possible new round of monetary accommodation by the ECB could increase it even further. There are two reasons why this is unsustainable in the medium-long term. Firstly, because it is fuelled by insufficient demand and high unemployment in the eurozone (the desired outcome of the policies of internal devaluation pursued in recent years). Secondly, because it is dependent on other countries running equally large current account deficits. Traditionally the United States have played the role of 'consumers of last resort', but it is unrealistic to expect them—or anyone else—to be willing to go on absorbing European surpluses forever. To get a feeling of the American mood, I recommend reading this scathing critique of European neomercantilism that recently appeared in the *Wall Street Journal*.

To conclude, the last thing the eurozone needs is a further dose of quantitative easing. What it needs is a fiscal expansion aimed at boosting investment and demand through direct injections into the real economy, bypassing a broken financial sector. Quantitative easing for the people, if you like.

Schizophrenic Confidence?

Original title: *2011 In Review: Four Hard Truths*
Published on *iMFdirect* blog on December 21, 2011

In his "four lessons", Olivier Blanchard, chief economist at the IMF, introduces the topic of confidence by explaining how perception matters for economic policies' success. It is interesting to examine Blanchard's point of view since, given his highly influential appointment, it represents the mainstream in economic thought. This perception is also confirmed by the fact that he is the author of one of the most diffused macroeconomics textbook in Europe. As anticipated in the previous article by Skidelsky, supporters of austerity believe that "only balancing government budgets and shrinking national debts will restore investor confidence." On the other hand, stimulus-supporters think that "without a large fiscal stimulus—a deliberate temporary increase of the deficit—the [...] economies will remain stuck in recession for years to come". Blanchard endorses the first side, as he clearly states together with austerians, that "substantial fiscal consolidation is needed, and debt levels must decrease." In the following article, though, he is also embracing— even if not too explicitly—the idea mentioned by Skidelsky for which fiscal contraction restores confidence: as he highlights that "the higher the level of

© The Author(s) 2017   **87**
R. Skidelsky and N. Fraccaroli, *Austerity vs Stimulus*,
DOI 10.1007/978-3-319-50439-1_10

debt, the smaller the distance between solvency and default," and therefore "investors start having doubts." Nevertheless, for Blanchard it is not all black or white. Investors, in fact, seem to be "schizophrenic," as "they react positively to news of fiscal consolidation, but then react negatively later, when consolidation leads to lower growth—which it often does". Blanchard's sentence is a brilliant synthesis of the two positions, as the first part reflects the pro-austerity belief that fiscal consolidation restores confidence, while the second one displays the stimulus-supporters thesis for which confidence is damaged by the same consolidation for its negative effects on growth.

By **Olivier Blanchard**

What a Difference a Year Makes …

We started 2011 in recovery mode, admittedly weak and unbalanced, but nevertheless there was hope. The issues appeared more tractable: how to deal with excessive housing debt in the United States, how to deal with adjustment in countries at the periphery of the Euro area, how to handle volatile capital inflows to emerging economies, and how to improve financial sector regulation.

It was a long agenda, but one that appeared within reach.

Yet, as the year draws to a close, the recovery in many advanced economies is at a standstill, with some investors even exploring the implications of a potential breakup of the euro zone, and the real possibility that conditions may be worse than we saw in 2008.

I draw **four main lessons** [this and the rest of the bold by Blanchard] from what has happened.

• First, post the 2008–2009 crisis, the world economy is pregnant with multiple equilibria—**self-fulfilling outcomes of pessimism or optimism, with major macroeconomic implications.**

[…]

What has become clearer this year is that liquidity problems, and associated runs, can also affect governments. Like banks, government liabilities are much more liquid than their assets—largely future tax receipts. If investors believe they are solvent, they can borrow at a riskless rate; if investors start having doubts, and require a higher rate, the high rate may well lead to default. The higher the level of debt, the smaller the distance between solvency and default, and the smaller the distance between the interest rate associated with solvency and the interest rate associated with default. Italy is the current poster child, but we should be under no illusion: in the post-crisis environment of high government debt and worried investors, many governments are exposed. Without adequate liquidity provision to ensure that interest rates remain reasonable, the danger is there.

• Second, **incomplete or partial policy measures can make things worse.**

We saw how perceptions often got worse after high-level meetings promised a solution, but delivered only half of one. Or when plans announced with fanfare turned out to be insufficient or hit practical obstacles.

The reason, I believe, is that these meetings and plans revealed the limits of policy, typically because of disagreements across countries. Before the fact, investors could not be certain, but put some probability on the ability of players to deliver. The high-profile attempts made it clear that delivery simply could not be fully achieved, at least not then. Clearly, the proverb, "Better to have tried and failed, than not to have tried at all," does not always apply.

• Third, **financial investors are schizophrenic about fiscal consolidation and growth.**

They react positively to news of fiscal consolidation, but then react negatively later, when consolidation leads to lower growth—which it often does. Some preliminary estimates that the IMF is working on suggest that it does not take large multipliers for the joint effects of fiscal consolidation and the implied lower growth to lead in the end to an increase, not a decrease, in risk spreads on government bonds. To the extent that governments feel they have to respond to markets, they may be induced to consolidate too fast, even from the narrow point of view of debt sustainability.

I should be clear here. Substantial fiscal consolidation is needed, and debt levels must decrease. But it should be, in the words of Angela

Merkel, a marathon rather than a sprint. It will take more than two decades to return to prudent levels of debt. There is a proverb that actually applies here too: "slow and steady wins the race."

• Fourth, **perception molds reality**.

Right or wrong, conceptual frames change with events. And once they have changed, there is no going back. For example, nothing much happened in Italy over the summer. But, once Italy was perceived as at risk, this perception did not go away. And perceptions matter: once the "real money" investors have left a market, they do not come back overnight.

A further example: not much happened to change the economic situation in the Euro zone in the second half of the year. But once markets and commentators started to mention the possible breakup of Euro, the perception remained and it also will not easily go away. Many financial investors are busy constructing strategies in case it happens.

Put these four factors together, and **you can explain why the year ends much worse than it started**.

Is all hope lost? No, but putting the recovery back on track will be harder than it was a year ago. It will take credible but realistic fiscal consolidation plans. It will take liquidity provision to avoid multiple equilibria. It will take plans that are not only announced, but implemented. And it will take much more effective collaboration among all involved.

I am hopeful it will happen. The alternative is just too unattractive.

Part IV

Austerity vs Stimulus in the UK

In this part we explore the Austerity vs Stimulus debate in the United Kingdom. It starts with two letters by prominent economists: one—published on *The Sunday Times*—encouraging the government to implement an austerity plan; the other one—published on *The Financial Times*—criticizes this.

The second chapter of the part looks at two debates: the first between the UK Secretary of State for Business, Innovation and Skills, Vince Cable and David Blanchflower and Robert Skidelsky; the second, between Skidelsky and the economic historians Niall Ferguson (Harvard University), following the discussions on public debt during 2015 Britain's general elections. The discussion on confidence introduced in the previous sections should be useful for the reader to understand and make up her/his own opinion on the current debate on fiscal policies. Confidence in fact, as the following section shows, is still at the center of the British debate for both the two sides.

Austerity for the UK

Original title: *UK economy cries out for credible rescue plan.*
Published on *The Sunday Times* on February 14, 2010.

By **Tim Besley et al.**

It is now clear that the UK economy entered the recession with a large structural budget deficit. As a result the UK's budget deficit is now the largest in our peacetime history and among the largest in the developed world.

In these circumstances a credible medium-term fiscal consolidation plan would make a sustainable recovery more likely.

In the absence of a credible plan, there is a risk that a loss of confidence in the UK's economic policy framework will contribute to higher long-term interest rates and/or currency instability, which could undermine the recovery.

In order to minimise this risk and support a sustainable recovery, the next government should set out a detailed plan to reduce the structural budget deficit more quickly than set out in the 2009 pre-budget report.

© The Author(s) 2017
R. Skidelsky and N. Fraccaroli, *Austerity vs Stimulus*,
DOI 10.1007/978-3-319-50439-1_11

The exact timing of measures should be sensitive to developments in the economy, particularly the fragility of the recovery. However, in order to be credible, the government's goal should be to eliminate the structural current budget deficit over the course of a parliament, and there is a compelling case, all else being equal, for the first measures beginning to take effect in the 2010–2011 fiscal year.

The bulk of this fiscal consolidation should be borne by reductions in government spending, but that process should be mindful of its impact on society's more vulnerable groups. Tax increases should be broad-based and minimise damaging increases in marginal tax rates on employment and investment.

In order to restore trust in the fiscal framework, the government should also introduce more independence into the generation of fiscal forecasts and the scrutiny of the government's performance against its stated fiscal goals.

Letter signed by:

1. **Tim Besley**, London School of Economics; 2. **Sir Howard Davies**, London School of Economics; 3. **Charles Goodhart**, London School of Economics; 4. **Albert Marcet**, London School of Economics; 5. **Christopher Pissarides**, London School of Economics; 6. **Danny Quah**, London School of Economics; 7. **Meghnad Desai** London School of Economics; 8. **Andrew Turnbull**, London School of Economics; 9. **Orazio Attanasio**, University College London 10. **Costas Meghir**, University College London; 11. **Sir John Vickers**, Oxford University; 12. **John Muellbauer**, Nuffield College, Oxford; 13. **David Newbery**, Cambridge University; 14. **Hashem Pesaran**, Cambridge University; 15. **Ken Rogoff**, Harvard University; 16. **Thomas Sargent**, New York University; 17. **Anne Sibert**, Birkbeck College, University of London; 18. **Michael Wickens**, University of York and Cardiff Business School; 19. **Roger Bootle**, Capital Economics; 20. **Bridget Rosewell**, GLA and Volterra Consulting.

Stimulus for the UK

Original title: *First priority must be to restore robust growth.*
Published on *The Financial Times* published on February 18, 2010.

By **Robert Skidelsky et al.**

Sir, In their letter to The Sunday Times of February 14, Professor Tim Besley and 19 co-signatories called for an accelerated programme of fiscal consolidation. We believe they are wrong.

They argue that the UK entered the recession with a large structural deficit and that "as a result the UK's deficit is now the largest in our peacetime history". What they fail to point out is that the current deficit reflects the deepest and longest global recession since the war, with extraordinary public sector fiscal and financial support needed to prevent the UK economy falling off a cliff. They omit to say that the contraction in UK output since September 2008 has been more than 6%, that unemployment has risen by almost 2% points and that the economy is not yet on a secure recovery path.

There is no disagreement that fiscal consolidation will be necessary to put UK public finances back on a sustainable basis. But the timing

© The Author(s) 2017
R. Skidelsky and N. Fraccaroli, *Austerity vs Stimulus*,
DOI 10.1007/978-3-319-50439-1_12

of the measures should depend on the strength of the recovery. The Treasury has committed itself to more than halving the budget deficit by 2013–2014, with most of the consolidation taking place when recovery is firmly established. In urging a faster pace of deficit reduction to reassure the financial markets, the signatories of the Sunday Times letter implicitly accept as binding the views of the same financial markets whose mistakes precipitated the crisis in the first place!

They seek to frighten us with the present level of the deficit but mention neither the automatic reduction that will be achieved as and when growth is resumed nor the effects of growth on investor confidence. How do the letter's signatories imagine foreign creditors will react if implementing fierce spending cuts tips the economy back into recession? To ask—as they do—for independent appraisal of fiscal policy forecasts is sensible. But for the good of the British people—and for fiscal sustainability—the first priority must be to restore robust economic growth. The wealth of the nation lies in what its citizens can produce.

Letter signed by:

1. Lord **Skidelsky**, University of Warwick, UK; 2. Marcus **Miller**, University of Warwick, UK; 3. David **Blanchflower**, Dartmouth College, US and University of Stirling, UK; 4. Kern **Alexander**, University of Zurich, Switzerland; 5. Martyn **Andrews**, University of Manchester, UK; 6. David **Bell**, University of Stirling, UK; 7. William **Brown**, University of Cambridge, UK; 8. Mustafa **Caglayan**, University of Sheffield, UK; 9. Victoria **Chick**, University College London, UK; 10. Christopher **Cramer**, SOAS, London, UK; 11. Paul **De Grauwe**, K. U. Leuven, Belgium; 12. Brad **DeLong**, U.C. Berkeley, US; 13. Marina **Della Giusta**, University of Reading, UK; 14. Andy **Dickerson**, University of Sheffield, UK; 15. John **Driffill**, Birkbeck College London, UK; 16. Ciaran **Driver**, Imperial College London, UK; 17. Sheila **Dow**, University of Stirling, UK; 18. Chris **Edwards**, University of East Anglia, UK; 19. Peter **Elias**, University of Warwick, UK; 20. Bob **Elliot**, University of Aberdeen, UK; 21. Jean-Paul **Fitoussi**, Sciences-po, Paris, France 4; 22. Giuseppe **Fontana**, University of Leeds, UK; 23. Richard **Freeman**, Harvard University, US; 24. Francis

Green, University of Kent, UK; 25. G.C. **Harcourt**, University of Cambridge and University of Adelaide, Australia; 26. Peter **Hammond**, University of Warwick, UK; 27. Mark **Hayes**, University of Cambridge, UK; 28. David **Held**, LSE, UK; 29. Jerome **de Henau**, Open University, UK; 30. Susan **Himmelweit**, Open University, UK; 31. Geoffrey **Hodgson**, University of Hertfordshire, UK; 32. Jane **Humphries**, University of Oxford, UK; 33. Grazia **Ietto-Gillies**, London South Bank University, UK; 34. George **Irvin**, SOAS London, UK; 35. Geraint **Johnes**, Lancaster University, UK; 36. Mary **Kaldor**, LSE, UK; 37. Alan **Kirman**, Ecole des Hautes Etudes en Sciences Sociales, Institut Universitaire de France; 38. Dennis **Leech**, Warwick University, UK; 39. Robert **MacCulloch**, Imperial College London, UK; 40. Stephen **Machin**, University College London, UK; 41. George **Magnus**, UBS Investment Bank; 42. Alan **Manning**, LSE, UK; 43. Ron **Martin**, University of Cambridge, UK; 44. Simon **Mohun**, QML, UK; 45. Phil **Murphy**, University of Swansea, UK; 46. Robin **Naylor**, University of Warwick, UK; 47. Alberto **Paloni**, University of Glasgow, UK; 48. Rick **van der Ploeg**, University of Oxford, UK; 49. Lord **Peston**, QML, London, UK; 50. Robert **Rowthorn**, University of Cambridge, UK; 51. Malcolm **Sawyer**, University of Leeds, UK; 52. Richard **Smith**, University of Cambridge, UK; 53. Frances **Stewart**, University of Oxford, UK; 54. Joseph **Stiglitz**, Columbia University, US; 55. Andrew **Trigg**, Open University, UK; 56. John Van **Reenen**, LSE, UK; 57. Roberto **Veneziani**, QML, UK; 58. John **Weeks**, SOAS, London, UK.

"Keynesian Austerity"

Original title: *Keynes would be on our side.*
Published on *New Statesman* on January 12, 2011.

By **Vince Cable**

If anyone doubted it before, recent months have proved decisively that coalitions are quite consistent with radical policy change. What matters now for British politics is whether the coalition government's economic policies deliver a sustainable recovery.

The most controversial part of the debate relates to the speed at which the fiscal deficit should be corrected. It is not, however, a controversy within the coalition. The structural deficit is over 6% of GDP—meaning that, even once the economy has recovered fully, the government would still be borrowing almost £100 bn a year. In September 2009, I argued in a Reform pamphlet that, in balancing the risks of too rapid adjustment (threatening recovery) or delaying it (precipitating a deficit funding crisis), the next government should try to eliminate this deficit over 5 years. Now we are in government, that is exactly what we plan to do.

© The Author(s) 2017
R. Skidelsky and N. Fraccaroli, *Austerity vs Stimulus*,
DOI 10.1007/978-3-319-50439-1_13

Despite all the controversy, the boundaries that define this debate are relatively narrow. The outgoing Labour government was already planning a fiscal tightening of 1.5% of GDP in 2010/2011. The difference between its deficit reduction plan beyond 2010/2011 and that of the coalition amounts to roughly half a per cent of GDP per annum: well within the forecasting error. Such differences, though not trivial, hardly justify the titanic clash of economic ideas advertised in the commentaries or a threatened mobilisation of opposition comparable to the General Strike. For all the protesters shouting "No to cuts", this electoral term would always have been about public-sector austerity, no matter who won the election.

As in many economic policy disputes, much of the ideological rhetoric conceals different forecasting assumptions—in respect of the cyclical, as opposed to structural, deficit; the influence of asset prices on consumer behaviour; the impact of the unorthodox monetary policy of quantitative easing (QE) and its interaction with the velocity of circulation of money; and the weight to be attached to business confidence and sentiment in financial markets. Amid such uncertainty, economic policymaking is like driving a car with an opaque windscreen, a large rear-view mirror and poor brakes. To avoid the trap of self-justifying, competitive forecasting, the government has subcontracted its forecasts to an independent body, the Office for Budget Responsibility (OBR). As it happens, the OBR has produced the reassuring estimate that, on plausible assumptions, growth should improve, unemployment should fall and fiscal consolidation should ease to safe levels over the 5-year life of this parliament. But even such an independent body can only point to a range of probabilities.

This lack of solid ground has failed to discourage serious people from invoking different economic philosophies to justify polarised positions. Increasingly, the debate is characterised in terms of John Maynard Keynes (in the "left" corner) v the reincarnations of his 1930s critics (in the "right" corner). Whatever their motivations, Nobel prize winners and other economists are lining up with party politicians to re-enact the dramas of 80 years ago, like history buffs dressing up in armour to relive the battles of the English civil war.

This politicisation is odd, because Keynes was a liberal, not a socialist (nor even a social democrat). He showed no fundamental discomfort with the then modest levels of state spending in the economy, which amounted to half of today's level as a share of GDP. Keynes's policies were intended not to overthrow capitalism but to save it from a systemic malfunction—the problem of insufficient aggregate demand.

Despite the mischaracterisation of Keynes as a friend of socialism, the ongoing debates are valuable insofar as they illuminate vital bits of theory and evidence. In a recent New Statesman essay (25 October 2010), Robert Skidelsky provides a very good exposition of the Keynesian interpretation of current problems and solutions. I would like to continue the debate but argue that Keynes would be on my side, not his.

The main theoretical issue is what determines investment. As illustrated in the OBR's forecasts, growth is expected to come from a large increase in private-sector investment, after decades in which ever-increasing consumption has borne too much of the burden of fuelling growth. Keynes, too, was consistently preoccupied with how to sustain investment as the motor of economic growth and employment. The specific problem he grappled with was what happens during a slump, when intended saving seriously diverges from intended investment, such that there is a pool of excessive savings, which, in turn, depresses spending and the willingness of business to produce and employ workers.

The orthodox response was that interest rates would fall, increasing investment and reducing savings, thus restoring balance. Flexible wages would operate to restore full employment. Keynes showed that, sometimes, this equilibrating mechanism may not work without government intervention to support demand, particularly when deflationary conditions pertain. During periods of weak expected demand, consumers and businessmen hold back from spending and reinforce the deflationary trend. This is the mistake that governments of the interwar period perpetrated.

Few would now deny that Keynes's insight was correct, and it was put to good use in the co-ordinated global response to the financial crisis 2 years ago. This response reflected an understanding that, while Keynes's original analysis was based on a model of a closed economy, today's investment/savings imbalances manifest themselves at a global level (with the UK, like the US, importing savings). Nonetheless, modern Keynesians claim to hear the echo of a long-dead 1930s controversy in the coalition government's policy of seeking an investment-led recovery and at the same time reducing state-financed demand, through cutting the government's current spending and increasing tax receipts.

Skidelsky concludes his essay by quoting Keynes, writing on investment in 1932, in the depths of the Great Depression: "It may still be the case that the lender, with his confidence shattered by his experience, will continue to ask for new enterprise rates of interest which the borrower cannot expect to earn ... There will be no means of escape from prolonged and, perhaps, interminable depression except by direct state intervention to promote and subsidise new investment."

In other words, there are times when only through government spending will the economy gain the growth in expected demand necessary to drag it out of a slump. The deflationary 1930s were certainly one such time. The question, however, is what relevance that insight has today.

Decision-making has to be evidence-based rather than dogmatic. At a macroeconomic level, there is now a wealth of experience of postwar fiscal adjustment in developed-market economies—more than 40 examples since the mid-1970s. This experience provides strong empirical support for the view that decisive rather than gradual budgetary adjustments, focusing on spending cuts, have been successful in correcting fiscal imbalances and have, in general, boosted rather than suppressed growth—the experience in Denmark in the 1980s, for example, as Francesco Giavazzi and Marco Pagano argued in 1990. A recent study by the International Monetary Fund determines that fiscal consolidation does, indeed, boost growth and employment but only in the long term (5 years or more) and may have negative effects in the short run.

The overall conclusions are non-Keynesian. What explains this? One plausible explanation, from Olivier Blanchard of the IMF, is that the Keynesian model of fiscal policy works well enough in most conditions, but not when there is a fiscal crisis. In those circumstances, households and businesses react to increased deficits by saving more, because they expect spending cuts and tax increases in the future. At a time like this, fiscal multipliers decline and turn negative. Conversely, firm action to reduce deficits provides reassurance to spend and invest. Such arguments are sometimes described as "Ricardian equivalence"—that deficits cannot stimulate demand because of expected future tax increases. While David Ricardo's name may have been misused to perpetuate an economic dogma—one popular in Germany—his mechanism could well explain behaviour in fiscal-crisis economies.

The Keynesian counteroffensive consists of several arguments. First, it is argued that "the myth of expansionary fiscal austerity" (Dean Baker, Centre for Economic Policy Research, October 2010) is based on extrapolating from the results of adjustment in boom conditions, or at least relatively favourable international conditions. As Keynes put it: "The boom, not the slump, is the right time for austerity at the Treasury."

[...]

It is true that the economy is still recovering from the economic equivalent of a heart attack, which took place 2 years ago. But the intensive-care phase has passed. Current conditions in the economy are far closer to recovery than to slump, with manufacturing, in particular, enjoying robust growth and survey after survey of business leaders indicating that they are planning for expansion.

Second, Keynesian critics are overly dismissive of the importance of keeping down the cost of capital (by maintaining the confidence of lenders). Skidelsky wrote in his essay that "even large reductions in interest rates might have quite small effects on activity". Yet this was not Keynes's view at all. In his open letter to Franklin D. Roosevelt in 1933, he argues: "I put in second place [after accelerated capital spending] the maintenance of cheap and abundant credit and, in particular, the reduction of long-term rates of interest ... Such a policy might become effective in the course of a few months and I attach great importance to it."

The coalition has had demonstrable success in this area. As the perceived risks of a fiscal crisis have receded, 10-year-term government bond yields in the UK have fallen from 3.7% in May to around 3.3% and are now closer to those in Germany and France than those in the troubled southern periphery of the EU. To see what the alternative might have been, you need only look at other European countries where yields have risen by 2% or more. Had this happened in Britain, with its eye-watering levels of private debt, the risk of a second dip into recession would have been very real.

A third and related point is that Skidelsky and others are inclined to dismiss arguments that rest on "matters of psychology" or "fatuous expressions of confidence". This is an odd criticism, as Keynes also relies heavily on the mass psychology of confidence induced by expansionary policies and on stimulating the "animal spirits" of entrepreneurs. It is especially odd in the wake of the global financial crisis, when loss of confidence in highly leveraged financial institutions caused widespread economic damage and at a point where highly leveraged governments are being subjected to the same degree of critical scrutiny.

One of the more worrying reactions of the Keynesian critics is their belief that Britain, in some undefined way, is immune from the kind of financial firestorm that occurred in the eurozone in April and May, or the repeated flare-ups from Greece through Spain and Portugal to Ireland since. Even some distinguished academic economists don't understand how volatile and vulnerable to speculative attack the capital markets have become. The cardinal error of the boom years was to assume that low, stable interest rates were a fact of life, when such conditions could vanish overnight. An important justification for our early action on the deficit was to remove any risk of a sterling debt crisis.

The fourth and final element of the Keynesian counteroffensive might be called the "plan B" problem: what if rapid cuts do have gravely depressive effects on economic activity and investment? Can a government, using fiscal discipline as a means of restoring confidence, produce an alternative plan?

There are several answers to this. The most important is that, while all sensible governments plan for contingencies, there is no reason to assume the need for a plan B or a plan C, because there is a credible plan A and every sign is that it is working.

Another observation is that tight fiscal policy can be expected to be offset by loose monetary policy. As Mervyn King said last June: "If prospects for growth were to weaken, the outlook for inflation would probably be lower and monetary policy could then respond." Indeed, our early recovery during the Depression is generally linked to leaving the gold standard in 1931 and enabling looser money. Though the effects of QE are not fully understood, it should be clear that it is effective—the fast growth of the cash economy since the easing began is evidence.

Furthermore, it is only through having a clear plan A that the government can claim to be well prepared if the economy takes an unexpected dip. As we have seen elsewhere in the world, the only countries that are capable of supporting their economies in a crisis are those that have the confidence of the bond market. Britain's credit is as good as it can be. Contrast this with our position going into the 2008–2009 recession: with a huge structural deficit and demonstrating no willingness to address it, the Labour government could afford very little stimulus (another point made both by me and by George Osborne in 2009).

It would be foolish to be complacent, however. I worry that the modern Keynesians are not bold enough and that the rather contrived indignation over the speed of deficit reduction distracts attention from more critical problems. We have, after all, just experienced the near collapse of the banking sector, the freezing of credit systems and the subsequent need to recapitalise banks leading to further credit restriction. The crisis was global but Britain's exceptional exposure to the global banks has left us disproportionately affected—if not quite as severely as Iceland or Ireland.

The economics of banking and credit crises was first explained properly by John Stuart Mill nearly 200 years ago. In modern times, the best analysis has come from Friedrich Hayek. As Meghnad Desai has put it: "The current crisis is very much a Hayekian crisis"—caused by excess credit, leading to bad investments that eventually collapsed. That is not to say Keynes was "wrong"; that would be as absurd as saying that Newton was "wrong" because he did not explain quantum phenomena. But we should be sceptical about Keynesian economists, however distinguished, who conspicuously failed to anticipate the financial crisis and now blithely ignore its consequences. Skidelsky's essay does not even make passing reference to the banking crisis, like someone dispensing advice on earthquake relief and reconstruction without any reference to past or future earthquakes.

We cannot ignore the causes of the crisis. That is why the government's deficit reduction programme, though necessary, is not sufficient. We still need to address the question of how to generate investment and sustainable growth. It will not happen automatically. Supply-side reforms will help: attracting inward investment; shifting taxation away from profitable, productive investment (as opposed to unproductive asset accumulation, as with property); reducing obstacles to productive activity; reforming corporate governance and takeover rules to encourage long-term—rather than speculative—investment; helping workers to adjust through training, retraining and a safety net of benefits.

But a central issue remains the high cost and low availability of capital in a low-interest environment. Real short-term interest rates are negative and real long-term rates close to zero. Capital is, in theory, cheap—and for those large companies that have access to capital markets or the confidence of the banks, borrowing has never been cheaper. But for smaller business borrowers that rely on the banking system, there is a continuing credit crunch, with high (often double-digit) interest rates, new charges or conditions, sometimes a blank refusal to offer any finance at all. Small companies are the backbone of our economy and, in their eagerness to deleverage, banks may squeeze the life out of productive enterprise. To remedy this problem requires an early move to counter the cyclical regulation of the banks and, in the wake of the Banking Commission, now sitting, structural reform of the banking sector.

The problem—of available capital failing to find its way into economic activity—goes wider than banking. Dieter Helm has described how there is huge, pent-up demand for infrastructure investment and abundant available savings, but the regulatory environment needs reform to reduce the cost of capital. There is what Keynes described as a problem of "liquidity preference", but it is not caused by lack of demand. Put simply, investors need reasonable reassurance that they will get their money back with decent, long-term rates of return and the ability to buy and sell their investment cheaply.

Keynes was right to argue that the state has a critical role to play in facilitating investment. Banking reform is one requirement, as is reform of the regulatory system to encourage private investment in public goods. Other innovations such as local tax increments and tolling can free up investment without undermining fiscal credibility. The government is already relaxing a little the deep cuts inherited from the Labour government in capital spending.

The serious debate for progressives should not centre on denying the need for discipline over public spending. If the British left follows Bob Crow and the National Union of Students to the promised land of the big spenders, it will enjoy short-term popularity at the expense of the coalition but it will also enter an intellectual and political blind alley. We need instead to reform the British state to create a banking system, incentives and institutions that will put safety first, not speculation, and will liberate new and sustainable investment. That is the challenge Keynes would have relished.

Britain's Confidence

Original title: *Cable's Attempt to Claim Keynes is Well Argued—but Unconvincing.*
Published on *New Statesman* on January 24, 2011.

By **David Blanchflower and Robert Skidelsky**

Vince Cable's essay [...] is the first, and very welcome, sign of a senior coalition politician being willing to engage in a serious public debate on economic policy. It is in a different intellectual league from the jejune meditations of the Chancellor, George Osborne. Cable has written a well-argued—but ultimately unconvincing—defence of the coalition's economic strategy.

His first, and perhaps least interesting, argument is that the parties are in agreement about a deficit reduction policy: the only question is the speed of reduction. This may be so, but a consensus is not the same thing as the truth. Cable argues that it is appropriate to begin to pay off the deficit "over 5 years". It is important to point out, however, that there is no basis in economics for the imposition of a time period. This

© The Author(s) 2017
R. Skidelsky and N. Fraccaroli, *Austerity vs Stimulus*,
DOI 10.1007/978-3-319-50439-1_14

choice of 5 years is entirely arbitrary, as, indeed, was the time frame of the Labour government's less austere fiscal tightening plan.

The only sensible course was—and still is—to commit to reducing the deficit at a speed and by an amount determined by economic circumstances. This would have the benefit of allowing decision-makers to avoid taking a premature view on the size of the "structural deficit". Cable says it would have been 6% of GDP even with "full recovery", but readers should know that there is considerable doubt about this number, which the Business Secretary brandishes so confidently.

"Look after unemployment and the Budget will look after itself," was John Maynard Key-nes's advice. This may not always be true but it is better than the coalition's current stance of: "Look after the Budget and unemployment will look after itself."

Paying off the deficit too quickly, on the basis of projections that even Cable concedes are highly uncertain, carries a far greater risk of a decade or more of lost output and social unrest and dislocation than a more measured path that is dependent on, for example, the economy hitting unemployment targets. When unemployment is far above any plausible "natural" rate, longer is likely to be better than shorter.

Cable seems to place a great deal of faith in the confidence-boosting effect of fiscal contractions. But the empirical evidence for this is far from convincing. An important study by Vincent Hogan (Scandinavian Journal of Economics, 106(4), 2004) finds that the increase in private consumption produced by fiscal contraction is not sufficient to offset the direct effect of the reduction in public consumption.

Another study, by Rita Canale and others, published by the University of Naples in 2007, concludes that fiscal contraction may be consistent with an expansion of aggregate demand if monetary policy concurrently leads to devaluation. But it is the monetary loosening, not the fiscal contraction, which has this effect.

In such cases it would be more accurate to say that economic recovery is possible despite fiscal consolidation. The question then is whether recovery might have been faster and more dur-able had fiscal and monetary policy both been expansionary. Cable argues that, had the coalition not acted decisively to reduce the deficit, Britain would have faced a "crisis of confidence" similar to that of Greece, which would have forced up the yield on government bonds. This is frequently asserted, but it is far-fetched. Even before the coalition's deficit reduction plan, the British government was able to borrow at historically low rates. Moreover, the US treasury bond rate is even lower than ours, without a deficit reduction plan. There are many reasons for these low bond yields, but one of them is surely the diminished appetite for risk, itself a product of economic stagnation.

In any case, Britain is not Greece. For one thing, Greece has spent more than half the years since independence, in 1829, in default; Britain has not defaulted once in that period (see Carmen M. Reinhart and Kenneth S. Rogoff's *This Time Is Different*, Princeton University Press, 2009, page 99). In addition, the UK has its own central bank and a floating exchange rate, while Greece is stuck in monetary union.

Greece is characterised by endemic tax evasion, a poor tax collection infrastructure, paro-chial patronage policies, corruption and huge delays in the administrative courts dealing with tax disputes. This clearly does not resemble developments in the UK. Granted, there was always a risk that "contagion" would spread from Greece to Britain. But the Conservatives had planned to slash public spending before the Greek crisis flared up, as a matter of ideo-logical conviction. Greece was the excuse, not the reason.

Cable then embarks on the foolhardy project of enlisting Keynes on behalf of the coalition's policy. First, some clearing of the air: Keynes never denied that economies would recover from depressions without help from governments. What he argued was that countries would not regain full employment without an exogenous injection of demand. Without it, the business cycle would go on, but at a lower level of activity.

In short, without sufficient "stimulus", the employment and growth effects of a deep recession are long-lasting and likely to be large.

History bears this out. The UK and US did recover from the Great Depression, which reached its peak between 1929 and 1931, but the recovery was not strong enough to take them back to full employment for another 8 years, when significant war spending started. Think, too, of the effects in the 1980s of the recession under Margaret Thatcher. UK unemployment was 5.3% in May 1979 and remained above that level every month for the next 21 years until July 2000. There was another big collapse in output in 1937–1938, as there was in 1987–1989.

It is not enough to cite recoveries now in progress, or to chalk up growth rates, which recently have started to slow sharply. The question is whether current and projected growth rates will be strong and sustainable enough to restore full employment within some relatively short period, such as the life of this parliament. That seems unlikely.

Moreover, Cable severely underestimates the costs of prolonged underactivity. We need to take into account not just the output lost during the slump but the potential output lost in the subsequent periods of mediocre recovery. By 2015, the loss of output in the British economy from these two sources might well be in the order of 10%. That is, the British economy might well be 10% smaller than it would have been, had proper Keynesian policies been followed. This needs to be thought of in terms of the rusting away of human skills through persisting unemployment and failure to build the necessary infrastructure. As such, the knock-on effects go beyond 2015.

Cable is right to say that Keynes thought that the reduction of long-term interest rates had a vital role to play in sustaining any recovery. But he denied that it could happen naturally on its own, because, contrary to Cable's interpretation, he did not believe that there was a "pool of excess saving" in a slump. There are no "excessive savings" during a slump because the excess saving that caused the slump has been eliminated by the fall in income. That means there is no "natural" tendency for the interest rate to fall: the fall has to be brought about by central bank policy. This was the main goal of the Bank of England's recent £200bn quantitative easing (QE) policy.

More importantly, Keynes doubted whether the lowering of long-term interest rates would be enough to produce a full recovery. Again, the experience of the 1930s bears this out. "Cheap money" started a housing boom, which pulled the economy upwards, but it was never sufficient to restore full employment. The reason is that if profit expectations are sufficiently depressed, it might require negative real interest rates to produce a full-employment volume of investment. This is Keynes's liquidity trap.

Although we are not yet in this situation, bank lending remains limited despite QE, especially to small firms that are unable to issue bonds. Hence the velocity of circulation has not recovered to pre-crisis levels because the banks are limiting their lending so that they can rebuild their balance sheets and firms lack confidence to invest.

So, what are the prospects for strong recovery in the present policy regime? Cable notes, correctly, that the Office for Budget Responsibility has produced the reassuring estimate that, by plausible assumptions, there should be improving growth, falling unemployment and fiscal consolidation to safe levels over the 5-year life of this parliament. This forecast is considerably more optimistic than the consensus and is probably subject to marked downside risks, both externally, from further unravelling of the sovereign debt crisis, and domestically, where demand looks weak.

The latest economic data shows a big increase in the size of the national debt and in the debt-to-GDP ratio. GDP growth is slowing, unemployment has started to rise again—youth unemployment is approaching a million once more—and real wages are falling. Job creation in the private sector in the most recent quarter was exactly nil, while the public sector culled 33,000 jobs. In our view, under present policies, unemployment is likely to rise over the life of this parliament.

Furthermore, business and consumer confidence has collapsed since May 2010. This is illustrated in the two charts (Figs. 1 and 2). The first shows Markit's purchasing managers' indices (PMIs) for manufacturing, services and construction. Despite the recent jump in the manufacturing PMI, the overall index for the month dropped sharply, with big drops in services and construction. Commenting on the figures on 6 January, Markit suggested: "Worryingly, the slide in the PMI all-sector output index from 54.0 in November to 51.4 in December (the largest fall in points terms since November 2008) signals a slowing in GDP growth to near-stagnation in December."

The second chart shows the Nationwide Consumer Confidence Index, which has collapsed since the coalition took office. It now stands at its lowest point since March 2009, and well below its long-run average. The strong rally in sentiment that took place from the middle of 2009 into the first quarter of 2010 has been almost completely reversed. An equivalent EU consumer confidence survey follows a similar path. So much for the improvement in "animal spirits" supposedly brought about by the coalition government's policies.

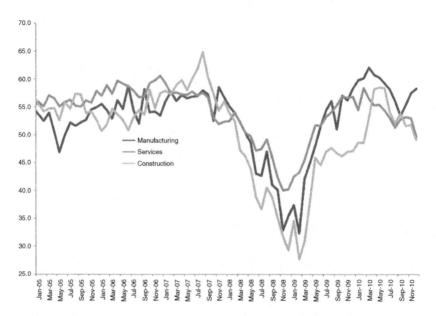

Fig. 1 Markit's Purchasing Managers' Index™ (PMI) for three sectors: manufacturing, services and construction (Jan. 2005—Nov. 2010). *Source* Markit.com

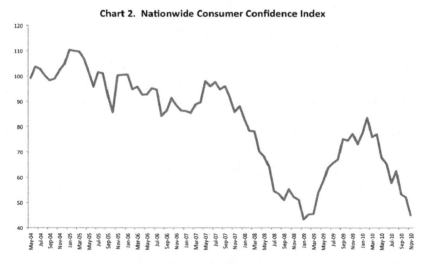

Fig. 2 Nationwide Consumer Confidence Index

We see no evidence currently that the UK economy is on course to "liberate new and sustainable investment". Cable agrees, and so do we, that the priority is to get the investment engine restarted. He cites the government's puny "green bank", which is bound to have minimal impact, as it has no money. We need a national investment bank that is committed to spending at least the equivalent of the planned cuts in current spending and ideally more than this. Cuts in payroll taxes—as the US has implemented recently—also look like a sensible way to raise employment.

In short, though Vince Cable's mind is working, the coalition is not.

The Economic Consequences of Mr. Osborne

The Ferguson-Skidelsky debate opens with an article by Ferguson which appeared in the Financial Times on 10 May 2015[1] [omitted] following the general election in which he claimed that the architect of the Conservative victory was George Osborne. Osborne's austerity policy had caused the British economy to flourish, contrary to the dire predictions of Paul Krugman, and the electorate had rewarded him. With a typical flourish, Ferguson wrote: 'Unfortunately for Mr. Krugman, the more he talked about the confidence fairy, the more business confidence recovered in the UK. In fact, at no point after May 2010 did it sink back to where it had been at the nadir of Gordon Brown's catastrophic premiership'. *Replying in Project Syndicate on 19 May 2015, Skidelsky said that Ferguson had ignored the damage Osborne's policies had inflicted on the British economy before recovery started, and blamed the Labour party for failing to defend the record of its own government. Jonathan Portes, then director of the NIESR also got involved in the exchanges with Ferguson.[2] We take up the story with Ferguson's rejoinder to Skidelsky in Project Syndicate on 19 May 2015, which led to further exchanges.*

By **Niall Ferguson**

© The Author(s) 2017
R. Skidelsky and N. Fraccaroli, *Austerity vs Stimulus*,
DOI 10.1007/978-3-319-50439-1_15

"If the facts change," John Maynard Keynes is supposed to have said, "I change my opinion. What do you do, sir?" It is a question his latter-day disciples should be asking themselves now.

Long before the United Kingdom's recent general election, which the Conservatives won by a margin that stunned their critics, the facts about the country's economic performance had indeed changed. Yet there is no sign of today's Keynesians changing their minds.

[...]

Let me restate why the Keynesians were wrong. In the wake of the 2010 British election, Skidelsky, like Krugman, predicted that Chancellor of the Exchequer George Osborne was gravely wrong in seeking to reduce the budget deficit. [...]

In June 2012, Skidelsky argued that "since May 2010, when US and British fiscal policy diverged, the US economy has grown – albeit slowly. The British economy is currently contracting. ... For Keynesians, this is not surprising: by cutting its spending, the government is also cutting its income. Austerity policies have plunged most European economies (including Britain's) into double-dip recessions." And, in May 2013, he reported that "The results of austerity had been "what any Keynesian would have expected: hardly any growth in the UK ... in the last two and a half years ... little reduction in public deficits, despite large spending cuts;...higher national debts... [and] prolonged unemployment."

By this time, groupthink had taken hold. Skidelsky approvingly quoted Krugman's claim that Britain was "doing worse this time than it did during the Great Depression." More than once he echoed Krugman's assertion that Osborne had been motivated by an erroneous belief that if he did not reduce the deficit, he might forfeit investor confidence (the "confidence fairy").

Just a week before the UK voted this month, Skidelsky speculated that voters, "still wobbly from Osborne's medicine," might "decide that they should have stayed in bed." Instead, the Tories won an outright majority, confounding pollsters and Keynesians alike. What could possibly have gone wrong—or, rather, right?

The last-ditch argument now put forward by Krugman is that the UK electorate was fooled into voting Conservative by a one-year pre-election boom, cynically generated by a covert Keynesian stimulus. It cannot have been easy for him to abandon his cherished macroeconomic model in favor of a conspiracy theory, especially one that two decades ago lost whatever explanatory power it ever had for UK elections.

But there is an alternative explanation: the Keynesians were wrong. "Austerity" was not nearly as harmful as they predicted. Fiscal stabilization may have contributed to a revival of confidence. In any case, nothing in modern British economic history told Osborne that he could risk running larger deficits with impunity.

There has been some sleight of hand in assessing Britain's recent economic performance. For example, Dean Baker took International Monetary Fund data for the G-7 countries' GDPs and made 2007 his base year. But a more appropriate benchmark is 2010, in the middle of which Cameron and Osborne took office. It is also worth including the latest IMF projections. And per capita GDP must surely be preferable to aggregate GDP (Fig. 1).

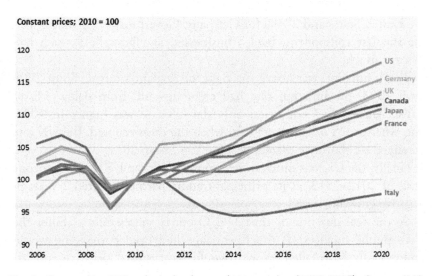

Fig. 1 Per capita GDP, selected advanced economies (2006–2020). *Source* IMF, World Economic Outlook database

No doubt, recovery in the UK began more slowly than in other G7 economies, except Italy. But there is also no doubt that the UK recovery picked up speed after 2012. Last year, its growth rate was the highest in the G7. According to the IMF, only the US economy will grow faster over the next 4 years, with the UK then regaining the lead.

It is wrong to assume that the UK could somehow have replicated the German or American recovery, if only Keynesian policies had been followed. The UK's position in 2010 was exceptionally bad in at least four respects, and certainly much worse than that of the US.

First, public finances were extremely weak, as a 2010 Bank for International Settlements study of trends in debt-to-GDP ratios clearly showed. The baseline scenario for the UK at that time was that, in the absence of fiscal reform, public debt would rise from 50% of GDP to above 500% by 2040. Only Japan was forecast to have a higher debt ratio by 2040 in the absence of reform.

Second, including financial-sector debt, non-financial business debt, and household debt the pre-crisis UK had become, under Labour governments, one of the world's most leveraged economies. In 1997, Labour's first year in power, aggregate UK debt stood at around 250% of GDP. By 2007, the figure exceeded 450%, compared with 290% for the United States and 274% for Germany. Government debt was in fact the smallest component; banks, businesses, and households each had twice as much.

Third, inflation was above the Bank of England's target. From 2000 until 2008, the inflation rate had crept upward, from below 1% to 3.6%. Among G-7 countries, only the US rate was higher in 2008; but, whereas US inflation cratered when the crisis erupted, the UK rate remained stubbornly elevated, peaking at 4.5% in 2011.

Finally, the UK was much more exposed than the US to the eurozone crisis of 2012–2013, as its principal trading partner suffered 2 years of negative growth.

So the real question is this: Did Osborne successfully stabilize the UK's public finances? If the Keynesians had been correct, he would undoubtedly have failed; growth would have turned negative and the fiscal/debt position would have worsened.

That is not what happened. Net government debt as a percentage of GDP had soared from 38 to 69% from 2007 to 2010. It rose under Osborne, too, but at a far slower pace, and is forecast to peak at 83% this year, after which it will decline. By 2020, according to the IMF, only Canada and Germany will be in better fiscal health (Fig. 2).

Stabilization of the public debt has been achieved by a drastic reduction of the government's deficit from a peak of just under 11% of GDP in 2009 to 6% last year. By 2018, according to the IMF, the deficit will have all but vanished. The same story can be told of the government's structural balance, which fell from 10% of GDP in 2009 to 4% in 2014 and should be just 0.5% in 2018 (Fig. 3).

This is an impressive performance in comparative terms. The US, for example, will still have a 4%-of-GDP deficit by 2020 on either of the above measures.

To be sure, the UK did not "deleverage"; but, under Osborne, the debt explosion was contained. Among advanced economies, only Germany, Norway, and the US achieved smaller increases in aggregate public and private debt/GDP ratios from 2007 to 2014.

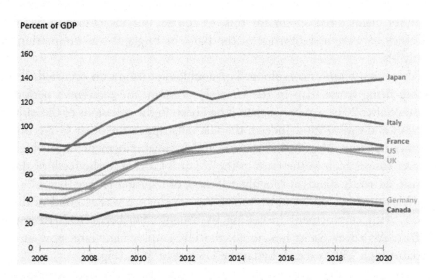

Fig. 2 Government Net Debt, selected advanced economies (2006–2020). *Source* IMF, World Economic Outlook database

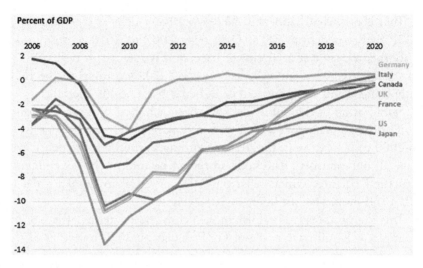

Fig. 3 General Government Net Lending (deficit), selected advanced economies (2006–2020). *Source* IMF, World Economic Outlook database

UK inflation was also brought under control, without the overshoot into deflation experienced by some developed countries. Osborne cannot claim direct credit for this, of course; but the choice of Mark Carney to serve as Governor of the Bank of England was unquestionably his.

Most important, no prolonged or double-dip depression occurred. Far from being worse than in the Great Depression, the economy's performance after 2010 was better than it had been in the recessions of the early 1980s and early 1990s. Indeed, the UK outstripped the other G-7 economies in terms of growth last year, and its unemployment rate, which never rose as high as the rates in the US and Canada in the teeth of the crisis, currently stands at roughly half those of Italy and France (Fig. 4).

Measured by job creation, too, UK performance was as good as the best, with employment increasing by roughly 5% between 2010 and 2014. As Jeffrey Sachs has noted, the UK employment rate, now at a record-high 73%, exceeds by far the US rate of 59% (Fig. 5).

The fact is that the more Keynesians like Skidelsky and Krugman talked about the "confidence fairy," the more confidence returned to

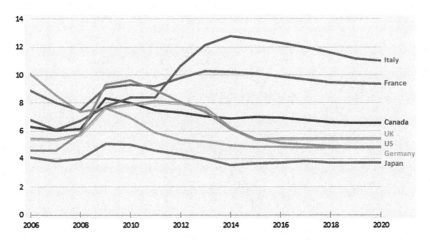

Fig. 4 Unemployment rate, selected advanced economies (2006–2020). *Source* IMF, World Economic Outlook database

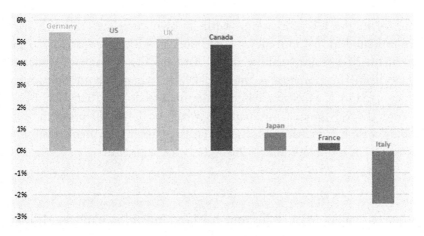

Fig. 5 Percentage Increase in Employment, selected advanced economies (2010–2014). *Source* IMF, World Economic Outlook database

UK business. One can argue about why that was, but it seems unlikely that Osborne's successful fiscal consolidation was irrelevant. There is certainly no evidence to support Krugman's repeated assertion that a

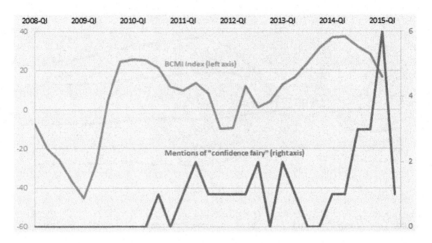

Fig. 6 Krugman's Confidence Fairy and UK Business Confidence (2008Q1–2015Q1). *Source* Grant Thornton, "UK Business Confidence Monitor," Q1 2015; New York Times

country in the UK's situation—with its own currency and with debt denominated in that currency—could borrow without constraint in the aftermath of a major banking crisis. (Perhaps the Keynesians prefer to efface from their memories the mid-1970s, when Labour politicians, encouraged by Keynesian advisers, attempted to do just that) (Fig. 6).

And the Keynesians' comparisons with the Great Depression were plainly risible from the outset. In terms of unemployment, even the recessions of the 1980s and 1990s were twice as painful.

[…]

Like Krugman (though his tone has been much less obnoxious), Lord Skidelsky has made the un-Keynesian mistake of sticking to an erroneous view in the face of changing facts. I look forward to the time when both have the intellectual honesty to admit that they were wrong—horribly wrong—about the economic consequences of Osborne's strategy.

Notes

1. Ferguson, Niall (2015) "The UK Labour party should blame Keynes for their election defeat", *Financial Times*, 10 May.
2. Portes, Jonathan (2015) "Right to reply—Jonathan Portes on Niall Ferguson", *The Spectator*, 11 June.

Niall Ferguson's Wishful Thinking

By **Robert Skidelsky**

Niall Ferguson begins his rejoinder to my rejoinder to his interpretation of the results of the United Kingdom's recent general election by citing an apocryphal Keynes quote: "If the facts change, I change my opinion. What do you do, sir?" But should the fact that the British economy grew last year by 2.6% have caused Keynesians to change their minds? Would it have caused Keynes to rewrite his General Theory of Employment, Interest and Money?

Ferguson seems to think so. I do not.

Keynes never thought that an economy, felled by a shock, would remain on the floor. There would always be some rebound, regardless of government policy. What he emphasized was the "time-element" in the cycle. With depressed profit expectations, an economy could remain in a semi-slump for years. There would be alternating periods of recovery and collapse, but this oscillation would occur around an anemic average level of activity.

Neither the suddenness of the financial collapse of 2008–2009 nor the sluggishness of the recovery since then would have led Keynes to change his mind; nor has it discredited the claims of today's Keynesians.

© The Author(s) 2017
R. Skidelsky and N. Fraccaroli, *Austerity vs Stimulus*,
DOI 10.1007/978-3-319-50439-1_16

While Ferguson includes several quotes from my past commentaries, he omits a very important passage: "All economies recover in the end. The question is how fast and how far." The task of government was—and remains—to strengthen whatever "natural forces" of recovery exist, if necessary by providing businesses with a larger market, and, beyond this, to offset the inherent volatility of private investment through a stable program of public investment.

My argument with Ferguson concentrates on two main points: the impact of austerity on the British economy, its impact on the budget, and the relationship between austerity and confidence.

Ferguson cites the 2.6% growth in 2014 as a measure of austerity's success. But the… real question is what austerity did to the economy over the 5 years of George Osborne's tenure as Chancellor of the Exchequer. It is now widely agreed that, far from speeding up the recovery, Osborne's austerity policy prolonged the slump (Fig. 1):

Simon Wren-Lewis of Oxford University has pointed out that UK austerity was at its "most intense" in the first 2 years of Osborne's chancellorship (2010–2011). The UK Office of Budget Responsibility, using conservative multipliers, calculated that austerity in this period reduced

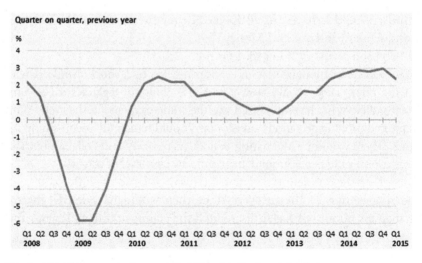

Fig. 1 UK GDP growth. *Source* UK Office for National Statistics

GDP growth by 1% in each year. That was the basis of Wren-Lewis's calculation that austerity cost the average UK household the equivalent of at least £4000. The economic recovery after 2012 coincided with the cessation of fiscal tightening.

Of course, coincidences are not causes. Keynesians cannot prove that the start of austerity aborted the recovery in 2010; that recovery would have come sooner if the pre-austerity level of public spending had been maintained; or that it was the reduction of austerity in 2012 that enabled the economy to expand again.

Nonetheless, the facts are consistent with Keynesian theory. Keynesians said austerity would cut output growth. Output growth fell. "[T]he Keynesians' comparisons with the Great Depression [of 1929–1932] were plainly risible," wrote Ferguson. In fact, real per capita GDP has taken longer to recover this time around. While it regained its 1929 level 5 years later, today, it is still below the 2008 level…

Keynesians also predicted that austerity would make it harder, not easier, for Osborne to hit his fiscal targets. Osborne said he would eliminate the structural deficit and have the debt/GDP ratio falling by 2015. Five years on, Osborne has failed to liquidate the deficit, no matter how you define it, and the debt/GDP ratio has risen from 69 to 80%.

Unlike Ferguson, Keynesians have a theory to explain why the targets were missed: If fiscal tightening makes the economy smaller than it would have been otherwise, it is much more costly to balance the books; and the attempt is likely to be abandoned or suspended for fear of social and political consequences. This is precisely what happened.

As a historian, Ferguson must know that it is growth, not austerity, that is most conducive to reducing the national debt as a share of GDP. Consider the following (Fig. 2):

In 1929, the UK's national debt was higher than it had been when World War I ended, despite (or because of) 8 years of fiscal austerity. Conversely, from 1945 to 1970, the national debt shrank from 240% of GDP to 64% after 25 years of economic growth, most of it "real" (inflation-adjusted). Likewise, Paul Johnson, Director of the Institute for Fiscal Studies, said in December 2014 that it was not for lack of effort that the fiscal deficit had not fallen further. Rather, it was "because the economy performed so poorly in the first half of the parliament, hitting revenues very hard."

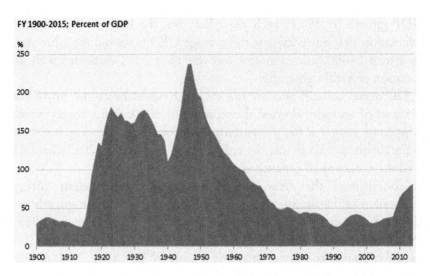

FY 1900-2015; Percent of GDP

Fig. 2 UK total government net debt (1900–2015). *Source* ukpublicspending. co.uk

The Keynesian argument, in sum, is that austerity hit the economy, and by hitting the economy, it worsened the fiscal balance. Does Ferguson accept this? If not, why not?

One of Ferguson's key arguments is that austerity was necessary to restore confidence. Apparently, the bond markets did not agree. Long-term nominal and real interest rates were already very low before Osborne became chancellor, and they stayed low afterwards. The government could have taken advantage of this to borrow at negative real rates to invest, as all Keynesians advocated. It refused to do so.

In the Financial Times commentary to which I was responding, Ferguson wrote: "…at no point after May 2010 did [confidence] sink back to where it had been *throughout* the past 2 years of Gordon Brown's catastrophic premiership" (my italics). But a graph that Ferguson himself posted gives the lie to this assertion (Fig. 3):

This shows confidence increasing from the low point of −45.3 in the first quarter of 2009 (the trough of the slump) to +25.8 in May 2010. It then went down, and did not regain its May 2010 level until the third quarter of 2013—an interval of 3 years. In other words, contrary to Ferguson's assertion, business confidence was higher in the last

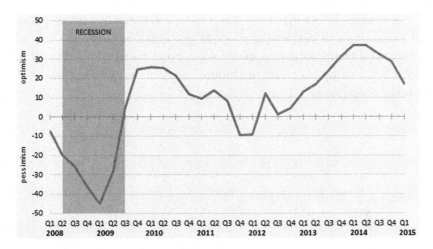

Fig. 3 Trend of UK business confidence. *Source* Grant Thornton, "UK Business Confidence Monitor," Q2 2015

6 months of Brown's premiership than in the first 2 years of Osborne's chancellorship.

A comparison with Fig. 1 shows that confidence closely tracks the actual performance of the economy. Austerity did not pull confidence up; it pushed it down, because it pushed the economy down. It takes a particularly perverse form of rational expectations to argue that confidence will be increased by policies that cause the economy to stall.

[...]

The austerity debate is of more than parochial British interest. Fiscal austerity remains the reigning orthodoxy in the Eurozone. With soaring private-sector and household debt, the current global recovery looks very shaky, so it is important to attempt an accurate audit of the policy responses to the last collapse before the next one occurs.

Ferguson is right that everyone should learn from experience. Keynesians cannot expect to have it all their way. Demand-side policies should be coupled with supply-side measures to improve skills, infrastructure, and access to finance, and Keynesians have been slow to understand that a government cannot increase the national debt without limit for a cause in which most people do not believe.

But it seems to me that Ferguson is more interested in making political points than in developing properly grounded arguments. Until he tells us why he thinks that austerity was a good thing, his critics will be forgiven for seeing his economic pronouncements as nothing more than political propaganda.

More Keynesian Than Keynes

By **Niall Ferguson**

[…]
Historical experience—including in the United Kingdom in the 1970s—tells us that financial markets are not always convinced by heavily indebted governments that promise to solve their problems by borrowing even more.

Responding to some early critics of his General Theory, Keynes showed that he recognized the importance of uncertainty in economic life, and consequently the difficulty of making predictions. "The whole object of the accumulation of wealth," he wrote, "is to produce results, or potential results, at a comparatively distant, and sometimes at an indefinitely distant, date."

But, Keynes continued, "our knowledge of the future is fluctuating, vague, and uncertain." There are simply too many things—from the "prospect of a European war" to the "price of copper and the interest rate 20 years hence"—about which "there is no scientific basis on which to form any calculable probability whatever."

© The Author(s) 2017
R. Skidelsky and N. Fraccaroli, *Austerity vs Stimulus*,
DOI 10.1007/978-3-319-50439-1_17

There was much that we did not know in 2010. We did not know if the UK's banking crisis was over; if its very large fiscal deficit (amounting to nearly 12% of GDP) was sustainable; or what the interest rate would be in 2 years, much less 20. The situation was so grave that no responsible politician favored the type of policies that Skidelsky argues should have been adopted.

In fact, at that point, the only real difference between the approach of the Labour government's chancellor of the exchequer, Alistair Darling, and that of Osborne consisted—as is clear from Darling's last budget statement—in the timing of austerity. In March 2010, Darling vowed to reduce the deficit to 5.2% of GDP by 2013–2014. Under his Conservative successor, the actual deficit in that year was 5.9%.

Skidelskyargues that "austerity hit the economy, and by hitting the economy, it worsened the fiscal balance." But that presupposes what he cannot prove: that a larger deficit could have been run without any costs.

All Skidelsky can offer as evidence to support this supposition is the view of the bond markets: "Long-term nominal and real interest rates were already very low before Osborne became chancellor, and they stayed low afterwards." But, if it were true that "austerity worsened the fiscal balance," the markets should have punished Osborne. They did not.

Likewise, if it was true that higher deficits carried no risks, but brought increased benefits, then the Financial Times would have been full of articles by investment-bank economists saying just that. It was not.

To be sure, I must acknowledge that I erred in one respect, which I am grateful to Skidelsky for pointing out. In May, I wrote that "at no point after May 2010 did [business confidence] sink back to where it had been throughout the past 2 years of Gordon Brown's catastrophic premiership." As Skidelsky rightly pointed out, confidence recovered from its low point in the first quarter of 2009, and reached a plateau in the first half of 2010. So I should have written: "At no point after May 2010 did it sink back to its nadir during Gordon Brown's catastrophic premiership."

But that does not alter my point that the more Paul Krugman talked about the "confidence fairy"—a term he coined after Osborne became Chancellor to ridicule anyone who argued for fiscal restraint—the more business confidence recovered in the UK. Although confidence fell somewhat in the first 2 years under Prime Minister David Cameron, it never approached the low point of the Brown period, and it later recovered. Nowadays, some economists seem to believe that pointing out a single factual error (out of more than 20 statements of fact) invalidates an entire argument. But, while it may cause a flutter on Twitter, that is not the way serious intellectual debate works.

[...]

A Final Word with Ferguson

By **Robert Skidelsky**

[…]

Ferguson's case against the Keynesians hinges crucially on the assertion that the Osborne package of 2010 was necessary to restore business confidence, and that it duly did so… He now admits that he was wrong—that "confidence fell somewhat in the first 2 years under Prime Minister David Cameron"—but urges in mitigation that a "single factual error" does not invalidate "an entire argument." In fact, Ferguson's entire case rests on this single factual error.

The graph below shows very clearly how closely confidence rises and falls with GDP growth. This explains why confidence fell to the low point that it did during Gordon Brown's premiership: just look at what was happening to the economy as a result of the global collapse. Indeed, the fit is even better than the graph suggests, because the GDP figures shown for 2011–2012 have been revised upward—that is, they were expected to be worse (Fig. 1).

Ferguson says that I cannot prove that austerity lowered UK GDP growth, or that it was responsible for the dip in confidence. And he is

© The Author(s) 2017
R. Skidelsky and N. Fraccaroli, *Austerity vs Stimulus*,
DOI 10.1007/978-3-319-50439-1_18

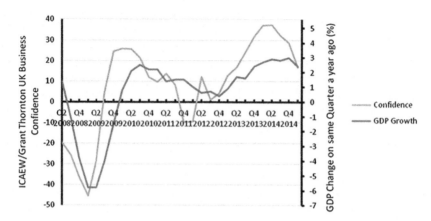

Fig. 1 UK business confidence and GDP growth compared (2008–2015)

of course right: Economists cannot prove anything. But that does not mean that people are entitled to talk nonsense. I have made an economic argument that taking money out of an economy in a slump will damage GDP growth, thereby damaging business confidence as well. I have provided factual evidence that this might well have happened. As far as I can see, Ferguson has provided no argument at all, while the factual evidence on which he relies to controvert my argument was wrong.

Here matters can surely rest.

A Stimulus Policy for the UK

This is a modified version of the article published in *The New Statesman* on January 16, 2016 with the title *The Optimism Error*

Until this moment we have compared theories and checked them against some economic data. Nevertheless, while we were able to analyse the performance of the austerity policies implemented in the UK, stimulus remained confined in the field of the theory, since it experienced no recent application in Great Britain. Consequently, talking about stimulus in the British context may sound a bit too vague, since the term does not refer to a specific application but generically to an economic expansion which entails the creation of a deficit. This can be done in very different manners though. As seen above, even the QE can be considered a stimulus policy, even if it may eventually act in support of fiscal austerity, like it did in the Eurozone. Such ambiguity can be account as one of the reasons for the diffuse scepticism toward the increase of deficit. The concept of economic stimulus has in fact many facets depending on the context. First of all, an increase in expenditure has very different effects depending on whether it regards exclusively current spending or capital spending (public investment). Moreover, since an expansion in capital spending is nothing more than an investment, it

© The Author(s) 2017
R. Skidelsky and N. Fraccaroli, *Austerity vs Stimulus*,
DOI 10.1007/978-3-319-50439-1_19

can have different outcomes depending on the nature of the expense: build-ing a hospital will not have the same effects as financing a war, for example. Therefore, to contextualise the role of a stimulus policy in the UK, we considered it useful to add an example of proposal of expansionary pol-icy for Great Britain. In the following article, Robert Skidelsky proposes the creation of a publicly-owned investment bank, based on the model of the European Investment Bank and of the German Kreditanstalt für Wiederaufbau.

This policy-proposal concludes this section of the book. We decided to dedi-cate the following one to the politics of austerity. As the political scientist Peter Gourevitch (1986, p.17) wrote, in fact, "policy requires politics".[1] And stimulus does not take exception to it.

By **Robert Skidelsky**

The Keynesian policy regime ran from the from the 1950s to the 1970s. It was overthrown in the 1980s, and unemployment prevention was confined to interest rate policy, run by the central bank, not the govern-ment. By keeping the rate of inflation constant, the monetary authority could keep unemployment at its "natural rate". This worked quite well for a time, but then, following the widespread failure of the banking system, the world economy collapsed in 2008.

In a panic, the politicians from Barack Obama to Gordon Brown took Keynes out of the cupboard, dusted him down, and "stimulated" the economy like mad. When this produced some useful recovery, they got cold feet. "Keynes," they said, "you've done your job. Back in the cupboard you go." I wrote a book at the time called 'Keynes. The Return of the Master'. A reviewer pointed out that the Master had returned for 6 months only.

Why had the politicians' nerve failed and what were the conse-quences? The answer is that in bailing out leading banks and allowing budget deficits to soar, governments had incurred huge debts which threatened their financial credibility. It was claimed that bond yields would rise sharply adding to the cost of borrowing. This was never plau-sible in Britain, but bond yield spikes threatened default in Greece and other eurozone countries early in 2010.

So, long before the stimulus had been allowed to work its magic in restoring economic activity and government revenues, the fiscal engine was put into reverse, and the politics of austerity took over.

But austerity did not hasten recovery; it delayed it and rendered it limp when it came. Enter "quantitative easing" (QE). The central bank would flood banks and pension funds with cash. This, it was expected, would cause banks to lower interest rates, lend more, and, via a so-called wealth effect, cause companies and high net worth individuals to consume and invest more. But it didn't happen. There was a small initial impact, but it soon petered out. Bank lending, an important index of recovery, actually went down as the institutions sat on piles of cash and the wealthy speculated in property, contributing little to the real economy.

So we reach the present impasse. Events have confirmed that a competitive market economy is subject to severe collapses and the effects of these linger in the form of elevated unemployment, lower output, lower productivity, and increased poverty.

But at the same time counter-cyclical policy is disabled. Monetary expansion is much less potent than people believed; and using the budget deficit to fight unemployment is ruled out by the bond markets and the Financial Times. The levers either don't work, or we are not allowed to pull them. So where do we go from here?

The Current Situation

The first thing is to establish where we now are. How much recovery has there been in Britain?

Economists try to answer this question with reference to the output gap—the difference between what an economy is actually producing and what it can produce. The OECD's most recent estimate of this gap in the UK stands at a negligible −0.017%. We might conclude from this that the British economy is running full steam ahead and that we have, at last, successfully recovered from the crash. And this is in fact the basis of George Osborne's triumphalism. His critics, including myself, have been proved wrong. His austerity policies have worked. Or so we are told.

But such a conclusion would be premature. Although we are producing as much output as we can, our capacity to produce output has fallen. This can be shown by comparing the current economic situation to where we would expect to be according to the historic trend.

From this perspective, championed by Oxford economist Simon Wren-Lewis, the position is far less rosy. Growth in output per person in Britain (roughly "living standards") averaged approximately 2.25% per year for the half-century before 2008. Recessions in the past caused deviations downward from this path, but recoveries had delivered above trend growth, lifting us back up to the previous path. One can say that the "business cycle" oscillated between errors of pessimism and errors of optimism. In other words, losses of output were temporary.

This time it was different. The recovery from the financial crisis has been the weakest on record, and the result of this is a yawning gap between where we are and where we should have been. Output per head is between 10% and 15% below trend.

We are faced with a puzzle. If the output gap is as small as the OECD believes, then the British economy appears to have lost much of its productive potential. It is no longer a case of demand falling short of supply, leaving a surplus of workers and capital equipment. The supply is no longer available: we have lost 8 years growth of productivity. Between 1971 and 2007 productivity growth averaged 2 to 3% a year. Since the recession started it has been close to zero. Why is it that the recession turned spare capacity into lost capacity? One answer lies in the ugly word "hysteresis".

Hysteresis

This is an idea borrowed from physics. If an insulated wire is wrapped around an iron bar, and an electric current is then passed along the wire, the iron bar becomes magnetized. Some of this magnetism remains even after the current has been switched off. A shock, positive or negative, has a long-lasting effect.

An economy experiences hysteresis, not when output falls relative to potential output, but when potential output itself falls as a result of a recession. What happens is that the recession itself shrinks productive capacity: the economy's ability to produce output is impaired.

The intuition behind it is simple enough: if you let a recession last long enough for capital and labour to rust away you will lose growth potential, on account of discouraged workers, lost skills, depleted banks, and missing investment in future productivity. By not taking steps to offset the negative shock of the recession with the positive shock of a stimulus, the Conservative government may have cost the British economy 10% or more of potential output.

The phenomenon of hysteresis is not necessarily captured by high levels of "headline" unemployment. In fact, low levels of unemployment may reflect low productivity growth, as employers prefer to use cheap workers to investing in machines: for example, unemployed workers may be re-employed in part-time or minimum wage, or zero-hour contract jobs. Much of the new private sector job creation lauded by the Chancellor is exactly in such low productivity sectors. The collapse of investment is particularly serious, as investment is the main source of productivity.

The challenge for policy is to liquidate the hysteresis—to restore supply. How is this to be done?

Blockage of Policy

An economic recession is precipitated by a fall in private spending, be it investment or consumption. It can be countered by monetary and fiscal policy, aiming either to stimulate private spending or replace it temporarily by public spending. On the monetary front, Bank Rate was dropped to near zero at the end of 2008; this not being enough, the Bank of England pumped out hundreds of billions of pounds between 2009 and 2012, but too little of the money went into the real economy. As Keynes recognised, it is the spending of money, not the printing of it, which stimulates productive activity, and he warned that "if we are tempted to assert that money is the drink which stimulates the system to activity, we must remind ourselves that there may be several slips between the cup and the lip".

That left fiscal policy. Fiscal policy can fight recession by cutting taxes or increasing public spending. Both involve deliberately budgeting for a deficit. In Britain, any possible tolerance for a deficit larger than the one automatically caused by the recession was destroyed by fear mongering about unsustainable debt. From 2009 onwards, the difference between Labour and Conservative fiscal policy was simply about the speed of deficit reduction. The contribution that deliberate deficit budgeting might make to recovery was never mentioned except by unreconstructed Keynesians.

So we now have a situation in which the main tools available to government to bring about a robust recovery are out of action. In addition, sole reliance on monetary policy for stimulus creates a highly unbalanced recovery. The money the government pumps into the economy either sits idle or simply pumps up house prices, threatening to recreate the asset bubble which produced the crisis in the first place. We already have the highest rate of post-crash increase in house prices of all OECD countries. This suggests that the next crash cannot be far off.

The Public Accounts Trap

From 2009 onwards the main obstacle to a sensible recovery policy has been the obsession with balancing the budget. A government can finance its spending in one of three ways: it can raise taxes, borrow from the private sector, or borrow from the Bank of England (that is, "print money"). Each has advantages and disadvantages, but public opinion has decided that the first of these—covering all spending by taxes—is the only "honest" way. In popular discourse, borrowing signifies a "deficit", and a particular horror attaches to deficits, because they suggest the government is not "paying its way". "We must get the deficit down" has been the refrain of all parties.

Printing money to finance public investment has recently been suggested by both the Labour leader and shadow chancellor, as a way to get round the borrowing constraint. Its advantage is that it wouldn't directly increase the National Debt, since the government would only owe the money to itself. On the other hand, it might destroy confidence in the state's ability to control its spending, and it would jeopardise the independence of the central bank. So printing money to pay for public spending should only be a remedy of the last resort.

It is right to be concerned about a rising national debt. But the way to reverse it is not to cut down the economy, but to cause it to grow in a sustainable way. In many circumstances that means deliberately increasing the deficit. This is a paradox too far for most people to grasp. 'Increase the deficit to reduce the deficit. What nonsense!' they cry. But it makes perfect sense if the increased deficit causes the economy, and thus the government's revenues, to grow faster than the deficit. If the economy is in the doldrums, practically all forms of government expenditure should be welcomed, as they utilise idle resources. In our present situation, with little spare capacity, the government needs to think much more carefully about what it should be borrowing for.

Public finance theory makes a clear distinction between current and capital spending. A sound rule is that government should cover its current or recurring spending by taxation, but should borrow for capital spending, that is, investment. This is because current spending gives rise to no government-owned assets, whereas capital spending does.

If these assets are productive, they pay for themselves by increasing government earnings, either through user charges or increased tax revenues. If I pay for all my groceries "on tick" my debt will just go on rising. But if I borrow to invest, say, in my education, my increased earnings will be available to discharge my debt. As Thomas Sargent, certainly no Keynesian, wrote in 1981 (Federal Reserve Board of Minneapolis, Research Department *Working Paper W*) "The principles of classical economic theory condone deficits on capital account."

Now is an ideal time for the government to be investing in the economy, because it can borrow at such low interest rates. But surely this means increasing the deficit? Yes, it does, but in the same unobjectionable way as a business borrows money to build a plant, expecting the investment to pay off.

It is because the distinction between current and capital spending has become fuzzy through years of misuse and obfuscation that we have slipped into the state of thinking that all government spending must be balanced by taxes—in the jargon, that net public sector borrowing should normally be zero. George Osborne has now promised to "balance the budget"—by 2019–2020. But within this fiscal straitjacket the only way he can create room for more public investment is to reduce current spending, which in practice means cutting the welfare state.

A British Investment Bank

How can we break this block on capital spending? Several of us have been advocating a publicly-owned British Investment Bank. The need for such institutions has long been widely acknowledged in continental Europe and East Asia, partly because they fill a gap in the private investment market, partly because they create an institutional division between investment and current spending. A British Investment Bank, as I envisage it, would be owned by the government, but would be able to borrow a multiple of its subscribed capital to finance investment projects within an approved range. Its remit would include not only energy-saving projects but also others which can contribute to the rebalancing of the economy—particularly transport infrastructure, social housing and export-oriented SMEs.

Unfortunately, the conventional view in Britain is that a government-backed bank would be bound, for one reason or another, to 'pick losers', and thereby pile up non-performing loans. Like all fundamentalist beliefs, this has little empirical backing. Two relevant comparators—the European Investment Bank and Germany's KreditanstaltfürWiederaufbau—show that, in well-regulated financial systems, such banks pay for themselves. Neither bank has had to go back to its shareholder(s) to raise fresh money to cover losses. The European Union is currently setting up a European Fund for Strategic Investment which, with a capitalisation of 21bn euros, is expected to lever 315bn euros of investment over 3 years.

George Osborne has rejected this route to modernization. Instead of borrowing to renovate our infrastructure, the Chancellor is trying to get foreign, especially Chinese, companies to do it, even if they are state-owned. Looking at British energy companies and rail franchises, we can see that this is simply the latest in a long tradition of handing over our national assets to foreign states. Public enterprise is apparently good if it is not British.

Britain already has two small state investment banks—the Green Investment Bank and the British Business Bank. But the Treasury are so obsessed with avoiding any increase in the deficit that they have deprived these newly-formed institutions of any power to borrow. This has crippled their investment potential. The GIB was capitalised with £3.8bn of public funds in 2012: it has so far invested £2bn. Now the government proposes to privatise the Bank, because 'it is necessary to move the bank off the public balance sheet if it is to arrange additional funding through borrowing'. And the same fate no doubt awaits the British Business Bank, set up channel money to SMEs.

Apart from its unjustified belief that public investment must be loss-making, the Treasury stance is simply an artefact of its insistence that there should be no net borrowing. It was to avoid this serious and crippling effect on public investment that Gordon Brown, as Chancellor, was drawn into large scale the Private Finance Initiative, when there were cheaper financing mechanisms available.

Setting up a British Investment Bank with enough borrowing power to make it an effective investment vehicle is the essential first step towards rebuilding supply. Distancing it from politics by giving it a proper remit would give confidence that its projects would be selected on commercial, not political criteria.

But this step would not be possible without an intellectual recovery of the distinction between current account and capital spending, the making of the distinction central to the presentation of the budget accounts,and the separation of the current spending and the investment agencies of government to guard against the first being mislabeled the second.

Note

1. Gourevitch, P. (1986) 'Politics in Hard Times: Comparative Responses to International Economic Crises', Ithaca and London: Cornell University Press.

Part V

What's Next?

In this book we mainly talked about business confidence, as the main argument used by austerians, particularly in the UK, to defend their stance. Nevertheless, as we have shown, confidence has little to do with economics, and more to do with beliefs which may or may not be justified. One of them is that if a government, like a family, keeps its house in order, by paying off its debts, it would benefit everyone. David Graeber points out the falsity of this thesis using a very simple economic argument: the accounting identity between the public and the private sector. Because of the symmetry between the two, if a government runs a surplus, the private sector will go into deficit, and vice versa. Given this, it is clear that reality is far from the simple story about being "economically responsible" often proposed by the British government. Debt (and therefore fiscal policy) has to do with redistribution of resources, and therefore, as Graeber shows, it enters once again the realm of political economy, becoming a matter of power.

The Economics of Debt

Original Title: *Britain is Heading for Another 2008 Crash: Here's Why.*
Published on *The Guardian* on October 28, 2015.

By **David Graeber**

British public life has always been riddled with taboos, and nowhere is this more true than in the realm of economics. You can say anything you like about sex nowadays, but the moment the topic turns to fiscal policy, there are endless things that everyone knows, that are even written up in textbooks and scholarly articles, but no one is supposed to talk about in public. It's a real problem. Because of these taboos, it's impossible to talk about the real reasons for the 2008 crash, and this makes it almost certain something like it will happen again.

I'd like to talk […] about the greatest taboo of all. Let's call it the Peter-Paul principle: the less the government is in debt, the more everybody else is. I call it this because it's based on very simple mathematics. Say there are 40 poker chips. Peter holds half, Paul the other. Obviously if Peter gets 10 more, Paul has 10 less. Now look at this: it's a diagram of the balance between the public and private sectors in our economy: (Fig. 1)

© The Author(s) 2017
R. Skidelsky and N. Fraccaroli, *Austerity vs Stimulus*,
DOI 10.1007/978-3-319-50439-1_20

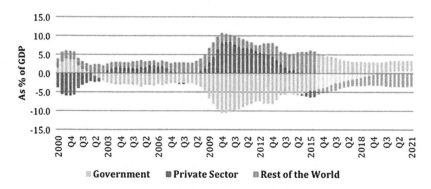

Fig. 1 UK sectoral balances and OBR forecasts (2000–2021)

Notice how the pattern is symmetrical? The top is an exact mirror of the bottom. This is what's called an "accounting identity". One goes up, the other must, necessarily, go down. What this means is that if the government declares "we must act responsibly and pay back the national debt" and runs a budget surplus, then it (the public sector) is taking more money in taxes out of the private sector than it's paying back in. That money has to come from somewhere. So if the government runs a surplus, the private sector goes into deficit. If the government reduces its debt, everyone else has to go into debt in exactly that proportion in order to balance their own budgets.

The chips are redistributed. This is not a theory. Just simple maths.

Now, obviously, the "private sector" includes everything from households and corner shops to giant corporations. If overall private debt goes up, that doesn't hit everyone equally. But who gets hit has very little to do with fiscal responsibility. It's mostly about power. The wealthy have a million ways to wriggle out of their debts, and as a result, when government debt is transferred to the private sector, that debt always gets passed down on to those least able to pay it: into middle-class mortgages, payday loans, and so on.

The people running the government know this. But they've learned if you just keep repeating, "We're just trying to behave responsibly! Families have to balance their books. Well, so do we," people will just assume that the government running a surplus will somehow make it easier for all of us to do so too. But in fact the reality is precisely the opposite: if the government manages to balance its books, that means you can't balance yours.

You may be objecting at this point: but why does anybody have to be in debt? Why can't everybody just balance their budgets? Governments, households, corporations … Everyone lives within their means and nobody ends up owing anything. Why can't we just do that?

Well there's an answer to that too: then there wouldn't be any money. This is another thing everybody knows but no one really wants to talk about. Money is debt. Banknotes are just so many circulating IOUs. (If you don't believe me, look at any banknote in your pocket. It says: "I promise to pay the bearer on demand the sum of five pounds." See? It's an IOU.) Pounds are either circulating government debt, or they're created by banks by making loans. That's where money comes from. Obviously if nobody took out any loans at all, there wouldn't be any money. The economy would collapse.

So there has to be debt. And debt has to be owed to someone. Let us refer to this group collectively as "rich people", since most of them are. If the government runs up a lot of debt, that means rich people hold a lot of government bonds, which pay quite low rates of interest; the government taxes you to pay them off. If the government pays off its debt, what it's basically doing is transferring that debt directly to you, as mortgage debt, credit card debt, payday loans, and so on. Of course the money is still owed to the same rich people. But now those rich people can collect much higher rates of interest.

But if you push all the debt on to those least able to pay, something does eventually have to give. There were three times in recent decades when the government ran a surplus: (Fig. 2)

Note how each surplus is followed, within a certain number of years, by an equal and opposite recession.

There's every reason to believe that's exactly what's about to happen now. At the moment, Conservative policy is to create a housing bubble. Inflated housing prices create a boom in construction and that makes it look as if the economy is growing. But it can only be paid for by saddling homeowners with more and more mortgage debt. Here's the Office for Budget Responsibility's own figures on what's going to happen to the cost of housing in the next few years: (Fig. 3)

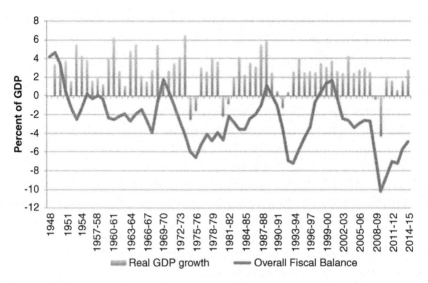

Fig. 2   UK Fiscal Balance and GDP growth (1948–2015)

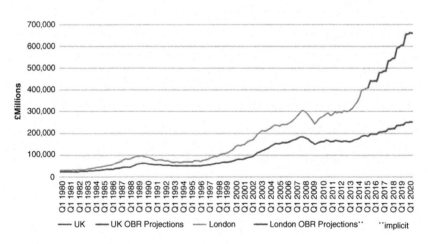

Fig. 3   UK house prices and OBR projections

The expression "takes off like a rocket ship" comes most immediately to mind. And here's what it says will happen to household debt as a result: (Fig. 4)

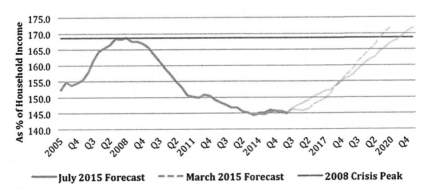

Fig. 4   UK household debt and OBR forecasts

This takes us right back to exactly where we were right before the 2008 mortgage crisis. Do you really think the results will be any different?

But something along these lines has to happen when the government runs a surplus. Everyone will just keep pushing the debt on to those least able to pay it, until the whole thing collapses like a house of cards: just like it did in 2008.

George Osborne's Economics: Austerity in the UK

The same straightforward argument proposed by Graeber is used in this open letter by Ha-Joon Chang, Thomas Piketty, Mariana Mazzucato et al. addressed to the Chancellor of the Exchequer George Osborne. The austerity policies implemented by the Conservative government do not have anything to do with modern economics. "Having the house in order", as Conservatives propose, simply means an increase in private debt, because of the accounting identity showed by Graeber. Economic stability, therefore, is far from being achieved through budget cuts, which would instead tie government's hands by reducing its leeway on future policies.

By **Ha-Joon Chang et al.**

The chancellor's plans, announced in his Mansion House speech, for "permanent budget surpluses" are nothing more than an attempt to outmanoeuvre his opponents [...]. They have no basis in economics. Osborne's proposals are not fit for the complexity of a modern 21st-century economy and, as such, they risk a liquidity crisis that could also trigger banking problems, a fall in GDP, a crash, or all three.

© The Author(s) 2017
R. Skidelsky and N. Fraccaroli, *Austerity vs Stimulus*,
DOI 10.1007/978-3-319-50439-1_21

Economies rely on the principle of sectoral balancing, which states that sectors of the economy borrow and lend from and to each other, and their surpluses and debts must arithmetically balance out in monetary terms, because every credit has a corresponding debit. In other words, if one sector of the economy lends to another, it must be in debt by the same amount as the borrower is in credit. The economy is always in balance as a result, if just not at the right place. The government's budget position is not independent of the rest of the economy, and if it chooses to try to inflexibly run surpluses, and therefore no longer borrow, the knock-on effect to the rest of the economy will be significant. Households, consumers and businesses may have to borrow more overall, and the risk of a personal debt crisis to rival 2008 could be very real indeed.

These plans tie the government's hands, meaning it won't be able to respond appropriately to constantly evolving economic circumstances, good or bad. The plan actually takes away one of the central purposes of modern government: to deliver a stable economy in which all can prosper. It is irresponsible for the chancellor to take such risky experiments with the economy to score political points. This policy requires an urgent rethink.

Dr Ha-Joon **Chang**, University of Cambridge

Thomas **Piketty**, Paris School of Economics

David **Blanchflower**, Bruce V Rauner professor of economics at Dartmouth College and ex-monetary policy committee

Prof Mariana **Mazzucato**, RM Phillips professor in the economics of innovation, University of Sussex

Jared **Bernstein**, Former chief economist and economic adviser to vice-president Joe Biden

Prof Simon **Wren-Lewis**, University of Oxford

Prof Victoria **Chick**, University College London

Prof Ozlem **Onaran**, Department of international business and economics, University of Greenwich

Prof Engelbert **Stockhammer**, Professor of economics, University of Kingston

Howard **Reed**, Director, Landman Economics

[*This version includes only the first 10 signatories. To see the other signatories published on the Guardian:* http://www.theguardian.com/politics/2015/jun/12/osborne-plan-has-no-basis-in-economics]

Conservatives and Keynes

If the failure of Austerity as an economic idea is today so evident, why do we still apply it? The answer lies in politics. Paul Krugman suggests that the left-right division on fiscal policy has deep roots. The right-wing bias for economic austerity is justified by their historical aversion to the government's expansionary policies. On the other hand, despite their liberal origins, Keynesian ideas are today endorsed by left-wing parties in Europe. The power of the idea of Austerity is therefore mostly political, and finds its expression in the many obstacles to a proper reform of the economic curricula in universities, which teaches the dogma of one single school of thought, the Neoclassical one.

By **Paul Krugman**

Tony Yates asks, "Why can't we all get along?" Lamenting another really bad, obviously political defense of austerity, he declares that

"it's disappointing that the debate has become a left-right thing. I don't see why it should".

But the debate over business-cycle economics has always been a left-right thing. Specifically, the right has always been deeply hostile to the

© The Author(s) 2017
R. Skidelsky and N. Fraccaroli, *Austerity vs Stimulus*,
DOI 10.1007/978-3-319-50439-1_22

notion that expansionary fiscal policy can ever be helpful or austerity harmful; most of the time it has been hostile to expansionary monetary policy too (in the long view, Friedman-type monetarism was an aberration; Hayek-type liquidationism is much more the norm). So the politicization of the macro debate isn't some happenstance, it evidently has deep roots.

Oh, and some of us have been discussing those roots in articles and blog posts for years now. We've noted that after World War II there was a concerted, disgraceful effort by conservatives and business interests to prevent the teaching of Keynesian economics in the universities, an effort that succeeded in killing the first real Keynesian textbook. Samuelson, luckily, managed to get past that barrier—and many were the complaints. William Buckley's God and Man at Yale was a diatribe against atheism (or the failure to include religious indoctrination, which to him was the same thing) and collectivism—by which he mainly meant teaching Keynesian macroeconomics.

What's it all about, then? The best stories seem to involve ulterior political motives. Keynesian economics, if true, would mean that governments don't have to be deeply concerned about business confidence, and don't have to respond to recessions by slashing social programs. Therefore it must not be true, and must be opposed. As I put it in [a previous article], "So one way to see the drive for austerity is as an application of a sort of reverse Hippocratic oath: 'First, do nothing to mitigate harm'. For the people must suffer if neoliberal reforms are to prosper".

If you think I'm being too flip, too conspiracy-minded, or both, OK—but what's your explanation? For conservative hostility to Keynes is not an intellectual fad of the moment. It has absolutely consistent for generations, and is clearly very deep-seated.

The Political Power of Austerity

Original title: *Austerity as ideology: A reply to my critics.*
Published in 2013 on *Comparative European Politics*, 11, 737–751.

This book has tried to answer many questions on austerity. What arguments is austerity based on, in what respects are they wrong, and where does the idea of austerity come from? We also explored why confidence has gained such an important role in the debate on fiscal policy and why it has to do with politics and ideology. Nevertheless, looking at the future of the Austerity vs Stimulus *debate, a question is still left unanswered: Why was* Austerity been so successful as a story? *Mark Blyth, author of* Austerity— The History of a Dangerous Idea, *examines different interpretations of this puzzle to propose, in the end, his own. What emerges in particular from his article is that economic explanations themselves are not enough to give an account of the debate on fiscal policies over the last 50 years. The* Austerity vs Stimulus *debate can in fact be totally understood only through the wider lenses of political economy.*

By **Mark Blyth**

R. Skidelsky and N. Fraccaroli, *Austerity vs Stimulus*,
DOI 10.1007/978-3-319-50439-1_23

Austerity thinking, and it is at base a form of thinking—a template designed to reduce complexity and clarify pathways to action—has been an unmitigated disaster for Europe. The policies resulting from this idea have produced above trend unemployment in the eurozone for 25 million people, with the periphery states losing between 20 and 30% of GDP over a 4-year period. And yet it continues.

The question worth asking, upon which we all agree, is why does it continue? I think it's more to do with the power of the idea of austerity itself than do my interlocutors (with the exception of Peck). Jabko, Thompson and Streeck each seek to downplay the ideological drivers behind austerity in Europe and offer other reasons for austerity's persistence. They each offer a distinct answer as to why 'it's not really ideology' doing the work and I make their responses to this issue fulcrum of my response.

Jabko (2013) sees political actors of varying ideological stripes using the financial crisis as an opening to do what otherwise would not get done. Let's call his diagnosis austerity as political opportunism, where ideas are justifications for instrumental plots and plans rather than causally important in their own right.

Helen Thompson, at base, sees governments' need for financial market credibility as the determinant of austerity as policy. Yields went up, debts had to be rolled over and budget deficits had to come down to get back to the markets. Let's call her diagnosis austerity as fiscal fundamentalism. Again, ideas are pretty much irrelevant.

Wolfgang Streeck sees the piling up of debts, both public and private, before 2008 as the means by which rich countries have postponed the crisis of growth that has been plaguing them for the past 30 years. Let's call his diagnosis austerity as payback,—payback for a failed attempt to substitute monetary growth for real growth [1]. His is the most structurally pessimistic view regarding our ability to end austerity.

I can agree with two of the three stances (Jabko and Streeck) right off bat. After all, what would be the point in denying instrumentality to actors? I certainly don't do so in the book [*Austerity. The History of a Dangerous Idea*]. Moreover, I am also inclined to accept the buildup of debt over the past 30 years (which as Streeck shows is mainly private and/or financial sector and not public sector) as evidence of austerity as payback. Again, as the book argues, the diversion of so much investible wealth into finance over this period, the consequent income skewing and leverage build-up, has indeed substituted paper growth for real growth throughout much of the OECD [2]. Given this, when the bubble popped, naked instrumentalism and 'give me my cash back' creditor/debtor politics came to the fore.

However, these answers still beg the same question. Austerity as policy—cutting the state's budget to stabilize public finances, restore competitiveness through wage cuts and create better investment expectations by lowering future tax burdens—has been an unmitigated failure. It has done more damage to the European economy than the 1970s and 1980s recessions plus the grinding slow recession of the 1990s combined. And yet it continues. Why? There is no attempt to stop it. Why not?

If this is creditor/debtor politics, then the creditors are being hurt just as much as debtors, and yet there has been no policy reversal. Surely the creditors cannot be so collectively dense that they can't understand simple the fallacies of composition such as the paradox of thrift? Meanwhile, evidence that telegraphs austerity's self-defeating character such as the various IMF reports from October 2012 onwards is brushed aside (for example, IMF World Economic Outlook, October 2012). Programs are lengthened and targets adjusted, but the underlying logic stays the same. Apropos Jabko's diagnoses, if this is just political opportunism, what on earth is the pay-off to the opportunists? Surely it has gotten to the point that the pay-off they get from setting up the European Stability Mechanism (ESM), or getting a weak form of bank regulation in place, pales into insignificance before the self-immolation of 20% of GDP and the perma-unemployment of a generation of young Europeans?

This is what pushes me to push ideology to the fore. 'Good' ideologies, to play off Jabko's term, are frameworks for action that have one defining feature: they are immune to empirical refutation. They persist and grow despite the evidence. This is why austerity is most of all an ideology. It is also why it is so dangerous. As I elaborate below, neither opportunism nor bond markets nor growth dynamics can explain why the political classes of Europe continue, despite all the evidence, to do such self-harm to their estates and to declare every little uptick in the data evidence of progress while discounting the error rates of all their prior predictions. The first law of getting out of a hole is to know when to stop digging. Europe is still digging and it seems unable to stop. [...]

Jabko's Inept Opportunists

[…] I find Jabko's contention that what's really driving events in Europe are political actors that 'saw an opportunity for the adoption of policies and reforms that they thought could only be introduced in a climate of crisis' to be half right. Yes, undoubtedly some of the impetus for reforms came from this direction. However, let us not discount the ideological drivers that work in parallel, and indeed enable such opportunism. Ideology's work goes beyond Jabko's diagnosis.

Consider the core message of Trichet's (2010) highly cited *Financial Times* Op Ed from 2010, 'Stimulate no More—Its now Time for all to Tighten', that 'the short term costs for economic growth [of austerity] tend to be very limited' and recovery will swiftly follow. Jabko's focus on opportunism would suggest Trichet's belief in expansionary fiscal consolidation is of secondary importance to its instrumental use. It enabled reforms that would not have otherwise happened. Yet what he shows is more blame avoidance than reform. It allowed, according to Jabko, the German government to argue for austerity, *for everyone else* in order to defend their own banking system from the liabilities that it incurred, and it likewise allowed the French government to talk a good game on austerity but to play the same game (essentially) as the Germans. I can only agree, but I don't see how this constitutes reform in any meaningful sense. […] Austerity has always been all about saving the banks while blaming the Greeks.

However, putting that aside, we must move beyond what ideas enable to how they limit the possibility set and guide action, which is why I think Jabko is only half right. While instrumentalist by deed, the direction of those actions, programmed with an austerity lens, becomes dangerously distorted. As I shall discuss more closely with regard to Thompson's diagnosis, the bond markets did not actually crave austerity. Hardly anyone can be found in the public record saying 'if French public spending isn't cut in half we will destroy the Euro'. Rather, as Greek yields spiked markets began to price in break-up risk for euro denominated assets [3]. And the solution to break-up risk is to have a credible central bank with a full lender of last resort capability at the helm; not a currency board with a liquidity pump and inflation target (the ECB).

Austerity as an idea led to policies that made things worse, not better, and they continue to be applied. It led to the identification of the wrong target (public sector balance sheets) and the wrong policy (simultaneous contraction instead of retooling the ECB). Instrumental and ideological logics are not alternatives, as Jabko lays clearly in his own work, so to separate them out here seems to lessen rather than increase our explanatory leverage.

Similarly, Jabko claims that not all austerians are conservatives, which is especially true in the German context. However, just as Thompson cautions that we should not generalize from either Iceland or the United States, we should also be careful when taking the left-right 'austerity for everyone else' coalition of German politics as representative of any state other than Germany. [...] There have never been any Germany Keynesians of note for the simple reason that as an export dependent high quality manufacturing economy whose 'de facto reason of state', as Thompson puts it beautifully, is to run a permanent trade and budget surplus, reflation simply hurts exports, so they don't do it. As such, the 'German Miracle' of the past decade owes more to a wage squeeze on export firm workers than anything else. Consumption restriction, not consumption expansion, is the German trick. However, that trick only applies to economies like Germany that can run a perma-surplus, and there are very few of those around. That less export dependent economies cleave to the same diagnosis of the problem again suggests to me again the power of the ideas as well of interests [4].

[...]

Thompson's Fundamentalists are Drunks Under the Lamppost

Apart from a few minor skirmishes over whether the Greeks and the Irish really volunteered for austerity, [...] disagreements [between Thompson and I] are threefold. The first lies, like Jabko, in the importance of financial market credibility as driving austerity policy. The second complaint lies in the 'easy ride' that I give the state in all of this.

The third lies, once again, in the role she accords for ideology, concluding that 'the ongoing costs of borrowing for most states will eventually make the ideology in this debate largely redundant' (Thompson 2013, p. 735).

Let me address ideology at the end of the discussion of financial market credibility rather than belabor the point again. Thompson's main claim is that in the eurozone 'governments have had to raise large amounts of new funds, and roll over, sometimes, huge quantities of existing debt, and relative perceptions of creditworthiness have shaped the interest rate at which they could do so' (Thompson 2013, p. 733). What the research for *Austerity* taught me is that this reading of events only makes sense if the markets demanded austerity, that is, *they bought into the idea* that cuts were what was needed, and they did not.

[...]

[Joe Wiesenthal] notes the crisis gaining speed in October 2010, with Italian yields[1] rising throughout 2011 as austerity budgets reached their apogee. That is, *as states cut massively throughout 2011 their yields went up and up, not down*. Note next the two circles when the yields start to dive. They correspond exactly to the first Long-Term Refinancing Operation (LTRO1) by the ECB when the Eurobanks ran out of local liquidity, in part thanks to austerity, and to December 2011 with LTRO2 was announced in late February 2012 as they ran out of US money market liquidity (Fig. 1).

Now note then the second circle, which corresponds to Draghi's 'whatever it takes' speech of late July 2012 and the subsequent unleashing of Emergency Liquidity Assistance (ELA) all over the continent as yields inched up again.

As Wiesenthal argues, and I agree, this is why the yields fell. Not because of austerity but because the half-central bank cum currency-board called the ECB finally started acting like a real central bank. Because of the emergence of a credible central bank policy to deal with contagion/break-up risk, which would blown-up the core country banks, the yield spikes abated. What mattered was central bank policy—not local budgetary austerity. Ireland's cuts in housing benefit, for example, had nothing to do with it, except make their situation worse by shrinking GDP and making their debts bigger and harder to pay off.

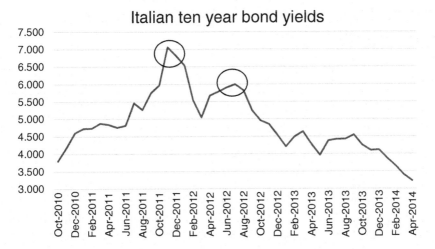

Fig. 1   Italian 10 year bond yields. *Source* Authors. Data: OECD (2016). Link to data source: http://stats.oecd.org/viewhtml.aspx?datasetcode=MEI_FIN&lang=en# Data extracted on 17 Dec 2016 16:09 UTC (GMT) from OECD.Stat. *Note* The chart above is a reproduction created by the authors of this book on the model of Wiesenthal's chart. For the original chart: J. Wiesenthal, Bloomberg, May 10th 2013

What is of course most ironic in all of this, to go back to ideology for a moment, is that in saying that he would do 'whatever it takes', Draghi did nothing, but the markets were reassured and yields dropped. Perceptions indeed matter, apparently more than fundamentals. It can't be the fundamentals of these economies lowering the yields as those fundamentals get worse each month. However, if all that is doing the work is literally the word of Draghi, it strongly suggests that credibility comes not from cuts, but from an intersubjective belief among market participants that Draghi will not allow a bank run around the bond market. In other words, *credere*—faith—belief—as the Italians have it—or ideas as I have it—matter most of all. Only in textbooks do market actors respond to fundamentals, and only when they read neoclassical textbooks or ECB instruction sheets, where state spending is always and everywhere bad, do they reach for austerity as the first policy choice. In reality, investors are like drunks under the lamppost: they look for the key where the light is. And in this case, the light shone from the ECB, not national budgets.

[…]

Streeck's Growth Crisis May not be a Crisis of Growth

Like any good Scot, I grew up Marxist. And then I grew dissatisfied with the 'easy boxes' of Marxist thinking. X is an example of relative surplus value, Y is over-accumulation, Z is spatial valorization. See it, label it and put it in the box. It's taxonomy more than explanation.

[...]

The ongoing financial crisis has reawakened these ideas within me and I struggle to quiet them. Someone who shares the same awakening doubts is Wolfgang Streeck, although he was more of a Weberian than a Marxist in his youth. What he gives us in his diagnosis of 'austerity and beyond' offers all of us the biggest challenge going forward. If he is right, then I need to apologize to a bunch of Marxists. However, there are reasons for thinking that he may be right, but not for the reasons he thinks, which means the Marxists may have to wait for that apology after all. That's the card I am going to play here. Time will tell which one of us is right.

[...]

Echoing and building upon Colin Crouch's work on privatized Keynesianism (where personal deficit financing through private credit took the place of public spending), Streeck shows that Crouch was only half right. Private credit substituted for wage growth to be sure, but public spending continued on the up, as shown in Streeck's Fig. 2. We have, as he puts it elsewhere, been 'buying time' with credit because we can no longer generate growth. The neoliberal reforms that were supposed to restore growth, the much-lauded 'structural reform' agenda, have failed to do so. Inflation, he also notes, is harder to generate in a neoliberalized economy as trade unions are either absent or compliant. Their ability to push costs up through wage settlements has disappeared.

In such a world, the ability to repress finance and get debt down through a liquidation/inflation tax is pretty much dead on arrival, and

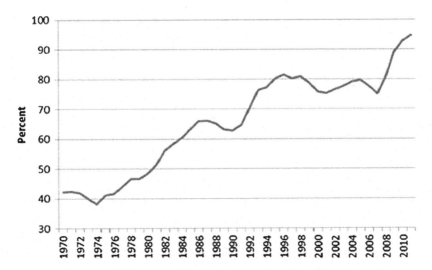

Fig. 2 Government debt as a percentage of GDP*, selected OECD countries** (1970–2011). *Annual Average Growth Rates of Selected OECD Countries, 1963–2010. **Countries included in unweighted average: Australia, Austria, Belgium, Canada, Denmark (from 1967), Finland, France, Germany, Greece (from 1971), Ireland, Italy, Japan, the Netherlands, Norway, Portugal, Spain, Sweden, Switzerland (from 1966), the United Kingdom, the United States. *Source* OECD Economic Outlook: Statistics and Projections (Database)

it seems that the markets, and their watchdogs such as the Bank for International Settlements (BIS), are beginning, as Streeck notes, to catch on. The markets wobble violently at the mere thought of an end to quantitative easing while they try to inspire another round of structural reform in the vain hope that this time it spurs growth. For Streeck, and the BIS, simply pumping cash into the system, monetary growth, is no longer enough. For as Streeck reminds us, echoing Keynes, free capital, which is what unlimited quantitative easing is in a positive interest rate environment, must lead to the euthanasia of the rentier class. However, this time around someone told the rentier class what's coming and they want to put the 'put option' of who pays for this lack of growth back on the rest of us.

The permanent austerity thesis of Peck (2013) may have deeper foundations than he fears if Streeck is right. If growth is dead we really, do need to 'start thinking about what that means' (Streeck 2013, p. 727) and my proposed solutions cannot work. But is he right? As I said above, I think Streeck is right about what he sees, but may be wrong about what it means. The key issue is whether the crisis of growth and the ballooning of debt he notes are structural (in which case he is right) or conjunctural (in which case I may not be right, but there may be hope). In closing, I want to make the conjunctural case for why the collapse in growth and the ballooning of debt can both be reversed because they are, at the end of the day, political and conjunctural rather than structural and economic problems.

Have a look again at Streeck's Fig. 2. It does seem to sit well with the Marxist story of a collapse of post-war growth followed by a neoliberal financial flowering in the 1980s and 1990s that held things up for a while, which has now popped in the crisis. However, if one discounts the last five observations, the average growth rate remains about 2.5%. It's certainly less than the post-war average of almost 5%, but several conjunctural factors can account for this.

First, the data set observed is OECD countries, which heavily weights European countries. Those countries have, since 1992, been deliberately lowering their long run growth rates by adhering to the Maastricht criteria and then joining a deflationary monetary union. Austerity politics today is the further and violent turning of the same screw. This is a conjunctural political choice and not a structural inevitability. Second, as growth has gone down, wages have stagnated with labor's share of national income now at historic lows, while income and wealth inequalities have reached historic highs in these same states. This gives rise to what might be called 'Kaleckian politics' where a concentrated investor class doesn't need to invest as they already own everything, with the result that capital formation lags and growth flattens out. This too is conjunctural, not structural, and so long as democracy persists this can be challenged. Third, the shift to a service-dominated economy, where capital cannot easily be added to inputs to augment productivity, clearly lowers growth potential. However, even this is only partly structural as giving up one's industrial base and/or encouraging it to move offshore are also political choices that can, in principle, be challenged.

Now return to Streeck's Fig. 2. The rise in government debt he plots is actually quite non linear. It actually fell from 1994 to 2006 as tax revenues increased and some states even paid back some debts [5]. Today's ballooning of debt is the cost of reinsuring the assets of the global investor class. This is why the public debt story is as much about political dynamics as it is growth dynamics. As Farrell and Quiggin (2011) put it in an essay in *Foreign Affairs*, the problem with Keynesian economics has never been the economics. It's always been the politics. Basically, there is no downside to the upside of a bubble for a democratic politician. None of the debt-obsessed Republicans that populate Congress today stood up in 2006 when US debt to GDP was 61% and said 'let's pay back the debt'. They said instead, 'let's have another round of tax cuts'. They forget that Keynesianism is symmetrical. When it's bad you borrow, when it's good you pay back. 'The boom, not the slump, is the time for Austerity', as Keynes put it [6]. What the OECD has been doing for the past 40 years is to award itself tax cuts, tax expenditures and declare more and more entitlements for the generation that has already made off with most of the growth of the past 30 years (Medicare Part D being the most egregious example) without caring a hoot how to pay for it. Again, this is politics. The rise in debt is neither linear nor inevitable. It can be challenged and the trajectory can be changed.

Next, look at Streeck's Fig. 3 for total debts across the public and private sectors of the OECD. Note how government debt, the great 'crisis' that supposedly necessitates austerity, is a tiny part of the picture. Household debt has increased, which represents stagnant wages and a credit bubble to be sure. However, it hasn't increased all that much relative to the villain of the piece: the financial sector. Indeed, fully a third of the total is financial sector leverage. That too was the result of politics. [...] The days when behemoth banks use excessive leverage and a free option on the public as a business model are ending. That debt is coming down too.

Now add to these *conjunctural* factors two others. The first is highlighted by Kuttner (2013). [...] Kuttner and I both note [...] how after the First World War creditors wrote policy. The result was Versailles, depression and war, as they all tried to get their money back at the same time as everyone's income shrank. [...] This time around, the allies wrote off huge piles of war and related debts. Indeed, today's creditor country extraordinaire Germany benefitted the most from this policy of debt relief, one that it now rules out for its debtors. But without such

■ Financial corporations ■ Households ░ Non-financial corporations ■ General government

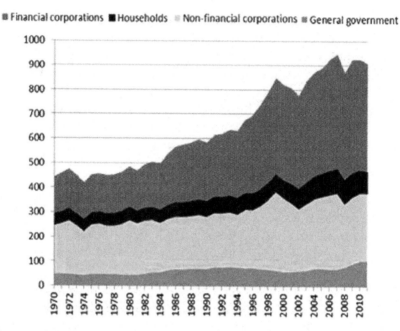

Fig. 3 Liabilities as a percentage of GDP by sector, the United States, 1970–2011. *Source* OECD National Accounts Statistics (Database): Financial Balance Sheets—Non-consolidated stocks

debt forgiveness growth is much harder. The post-war boom from 1945 to 1975 owed much to financial repression and high consumption due to rising real wages. However, what also made that growth possible was debt forgiveness, a forgiveness lacking today, but one that is once again, a political choice.

The second factor is a line from venture capitalist William Janeway's (2012) book *Doing Capitalism in the Innovation Economy*. Janeway argues against those saying we can't generate growth because there are no new game-changing innovations out there to boost productivity. This could be called the right-wing/supply-side version of Streeck's thesis. Janeway's reply is that making this call today on biotech, green tech, the Internet and other emergent industries is a bit like judging the impact of the automobile from the standpoint of 1924. I agree. Technology may be the liberal's 'rabbit out of the hat' for where the growth will come from, but it's not an unreasonable one historically.

Add all these factors together and we can begin to recognize that much of our debt and growth problem is political and conjunctural, not economic and structural, and we can try to change it. However, if we accept the view that it's 'all structural', and decide that we are doomed to no growth, we shall not even try to change our lot. I don't often close with Gramsci, but this time I shall. Perhaps a bit less 'pessimism of the intellect' and a little more 'optimism of the will' is warranted here. Growth can return, but only if we believe that it's possible to do so and we are ready to fight for its return. I shall hold my apologies to those on the structuralist side until that war is lost. The first battle we need to win in this war is the one against austerity. I consider my interlocutors, for all our differences, to be crucial allies in this ongoing campaign.

Notes

1. Seen in this way Streeck is perhaps telling Colin Crouch that, in Crouch's terms, 'Neoliberalism's Strange Non-Death' may be much more fatal then he anticipated, but only after the creditor classes have looted the corpse. See Schafer and Streeck (2013).
2. My favorite example of this being the 2003–2006 Citibank billion dollar advertising campaign 'Live Richly'.
3. This was something that came across to me in interview after interview with bond traders as I researched Austerity.
4. For Germany to be Germany, everyone else has to be 'not Germany'. Everything in the global economy sums to zero and yet the ideology of austerity demands that we all become 'more competitive'. See Austerity, chapter 5.
5. Clinton (1994–1999), Blair (1997–2001) and Prodi in the late 1990s spring to mind as obvious examples. However, note these are not examples of austerity. They are examples of paying back debt when there is growth, not when there is a recession.
6. Which is a bit of a misnomer as paying back debt in a boom is not austerity. Austerity is paying back debt in a slump.
7. According to Blyth, the Italian 10-year bond yields in period 2010–2013 depicted in the figure "mimic the behaviour of periphery bonds in general" (p. 742).

References

Farrell, H., & Quiggin, J. (2011). How to save the Euro—And the EU. *Foreign Affairs, 90*(3), 96–103.

Jabko, N. (2013). The political appeal of austerity. *Comparative European Politics, 11*(6), 705–712.

Janeway, W. (2012). *Doing capitalism in the innovation economy.* New York: Cambridge University Press.

Kuttner, R. (2013). *Debtor's prison: The politics of austerity versus possibility.* New York: Knopf.

Peck, J. (2013). Austere reason and the Eschatology of neoliberalism's end times. *Comparative European Politics, 11*(6), 713–721.

Schafer, A., & Streeck, W. (2013). *Politics in the age of austerity.* London: Polity Press.

Streeck, W. (2013). Will expansion work? On Mark Blyth, austerity: The history of a dangerous idea. *Comparative European Politics, 11*(6), 722–728.

Thompson, H. (2013). Austerity as ideology: the bait and switch of the banking crisis. *Comparative European Politics, 11*(6), 729–736.

Trichet, J. C. (2010, July 22). Stimulate no more—It is now time for all to tighten, *Financial Times.*

List of Suggested Readings

On Austerity

Alesina, A., Barbiero, O., Favero, C., Giavazzi, F., & Paradisi, M. (2015, January). *Austerity in 2009–2013* (NBER Working Paper. 20827). http://www.nber.org/papers/w20827.

De Long, B. (2012). Spending cuts to improve confidence? No, the arithmetic goes the wrong way. In G. Corsetti (Ed.), Austerity: Too much of a good thing? *VoxEu.*

De Long, B., & Summers, L. (2012). *Fiscal policies in a depressed economy.* Paper presented at the Spring 2012 Brookings Panel.

Helgadóttir, O. (2016). The Bocconi Boys go to Brussels: Italian economic ideas, professional networks and European austerity. *Journal of European Public Policy, 23*(3), 392–409.

Islam, I., & Chowdhury, A., Revisiting the evidence on expansionary fiscal austerity: Alesina's hour? *VoxEU.*
    http://voxeu.org/debates/commentaries/revisiting-evidence-expansionary-fiscal-austerity-alesina-s-hour.

Ostry, J., Loungani, P., & Furceri, D. (2016, June). Neoliberalism: Oversold? *IMF Finance and Development, 53*(2), 38–41. http://www.imf.org/external/pubs/ft/fandd/2016/06/pdf/ostry.pdf.

© The Editor(s) (if applicable) and The Author(s) 2017
R. Skidelsky and N. Fraccaroli, *Austerity vs Stimulus,*
DOI 10.1007/978-3-319-50439-1

Austerity in the UK and in Europe

Chick, V., & Pettifor, A. (2010, July). The economic consequences of Mr Osborne. Fiscal consolidation: Lessons from a century of UK macroeconomic statistics, Prime. http://www.primeeconomics.org/publications/the-economic-consequences-of-mr-osbourne.

De Grauwe, P., & Ji, Y. (2013, October 4). The legacy of austerity in the Eurozone. *CEPS*. https://www.ceps.eu/publications/legacy-austerity-eurozone.

Skidelsky, R., & Martin, F. (2011, July 31). Osborne's austerity gamble is fast being found out. *Financial Times*. https://next.ft.com/content/8f8888cc-bba9-11e0-a7c8-00144feabdc0.

Stiglitz, Piketty et al. (2015). In the final hour, a plea for economic sanity and humanity. http://www.feps-europe.eu/assets/4958a9ed-7b13-4477-a946-1b8e07dbd5b5/in-the-final-hour-a-plea-for-economic-sanity-and-humanity-ftpdf.pdf?utm_source=Monthly+Newsletter&utm_campaign=acbdfd430f-Financial_Times6_9_2015&utm_medium=email&utm_term=0_4aea2f6f40-acbd-fd430f-109320649.

Wren-Lewis, S. (2015, February 19). The austerity con. *London Review of Books*. http://www.lrb.co.uk/v37/n04/simon-wren-lewis/the-austerity-con.

Wren-Lewis, S. (2016, January 21). The dead hand of austerity; left and right. *mainly macro*. https://mainlymacro.blogspot.it/2016/01/the-dead-hand-of-austerity-left-and.html.

Index

© The Editor(s) (if applicable) and The Author(s) 2017
R. Skidelsky and N. Fraccaroli, *Austerity vs Stimulus*,
DOI 10.1007/978-3-319-50439-1

CPSIA information can be obtained
at www.ICGtesting.com
Printed in the USA
LVOW13s1913110817
544675LV00024B/1485/P